Despite threats of death and on her children, Esmie's fai

Beyond the Veil of Darkness

Esmie G. Branner

Pacific Press® Publishing Association
Nampa, Idaho
Oshawa, Ontario, Canada
www.pacificpress.com

Edited by Kenneth R. Wade
Designed by Dennis Ferree

Copyright 1999 by
Pacific Press® Publishing Association
Printed in the United States of America
All rights reserved

Additional copies of this book may be purchased at
http://www.adventistbookcenter.com

Unless otherwise noted, all Bible texts are quoted from the
King James Version.

Library of Congress Cataloging-in-Publication Data

Branner, Esmie G. (Esmie Glenora), 1960-
    Beyond the veil of darkness : despite threats of death and
    separation from her children, Esmie's faith took her— / Esmie G.
    Branner.
        p.   cm.
    ISBN 0-8163-1713-5 (pkb.)
    1. Branner, Esmie G. (Esmie Glenora) 1960-   . 2. Christian
biography. 3. Interfaith marriage—United States. 4. Interfaith
marriage—Saudi Arabia. 5. Christianity and other religions—Islam.
6. Islam—Relations—Christianity.   I. Title.
BR1725.B6827A3 1999
270. 8'25'092—dc21
    [b]   98-32389
                                                                CIP

02 03 • 6 5

Dedication

This book is dedicated to my children, Javid, Taariq, Adam, Aisha, and Zaina.

Children, you have nothing to fear for the future lest you forget the way God has led us in the past. Love God and others, be obedient and faithful to our Lord and Savior, Jesus Christ. Then and only then will you inherit the kingdom of heaven, and our joy will be full and complete.

Contents

Acknowledgments

To my brothers and sisters, Dorothy, Derick, Jeff, and Merlene; Janet and Neville Harrington, Stanley, Julie, and Marlon. Thank you for your prayers, love, and support.

To my niece, Denise, thank you for the time you took to type up the first draft of this story. Carl Fletcher, thank you for the articles and for exposing this story. Tamah Henley Curry, big thanks for the help and advice in constructing this book. To all my friends who encouraged me, thank you.

To my darling Mother, a true mother in Zion, thank you for the faith you have always exhibited and especially for your prayers.

To my husband, my best friend, Arthur Branner II, thank you for loving me and appreciating me. You are more than a gift of Creation, much more than what I had asked the Lord for, and a true priest in our home.

Thank you, God, for the wonderful testimony that you entrusted to me.

chapter 1

A New Beginning

It was a bright and sunny morning. As I awoke to face the day on which I fully expected to die, my heart was nonetheless rejoicing in my new experience with the Lord. I reflected on the beautiful candlelight Communion service of the night before. Everything seemed so perfect. Everything except the reality that the forces of evil were working against me and the threat of death hung over my head. For the first time in my life I was about to put all my trust in the Lord—a person I had never seen. Yet I knew there was no other way to find out the reality of God.

So often, as followers of Christ, we only allow Him to do the things that seem possible to us, those things that can be seen and explained by our own logic. But when we ask God to do the impossible, we sometimes withdraw our faith before God can act, and we never get to see Him and know Him well enough to build our faith. When Jacob wrestled with God, he never let go until he received his blessing from God (Genesis 32:24-30). So I had come to the breaking place where I knew that I had to either hold on and prove God or let go and never know of His true existence in my life.

It was a very tough decision. My life hung in the balance.

I did not want to die, and I told the Lord that I would rather live. I petitioned that God would save my children in His kingdom. I had made the most important decision of my life, and I was resolved that, even in the face of death, I could not and would not go back on my word.

The prospect of losing my husband and of never seeing my three sons and two daughters again was all too real as I planned to make good on the single most significant commitment to anything and anyone that I had made up to this point—a decision that would forever change my life and that of my husband and children. But I had to go through with my plans; I had learned too much and had come too far to abandon the Lord Jesus.

My mind had been made up for several weeks before I could bring myself to tell my husband. When I did, Mohamed seemingly underwent a complete personality change. He threatened to divorce me and to take the children from me. When I told him that I needed dresses for church, he withdrew all the money from our bank account. Coming to Christ made me realize how naked I really was, not only spiritually but literally too. I found nothing in my closet that was suitable for a Christian to wear. My good clothes were limited to either party or nightclub wear, and my casual clothes were not the kind that I could feel comfortable wearing to church. I believe that whatever we wear should honor God and speak of the relationship we are having with Jesus. I was virtually naked and penniless.

A few days before the baptism, Mohamed showed me the knife that he intended to run through my heart if I insisted on putting the family through this ordeal. He stopped buying food and provided only the bare necessities.

In spite of all this, God's promise that our bread and water would be sure sustained me, and I determined in my heart to secretly teach the children about the true God and tell them Bible stories. They loved it and always wanted to hear more.

Mohamed's threats did not deter me; I had decided to be baptized, and I was determined to make that decision a reality even if it was the last thing I ever did. I found that, as I studied the Word of God, I was being empowered with strength to continue on. However, there was a hint of fear in the air. What if Jesus didn't choose to spare my life? Who would raise my children and teach them of God? I experienced a tug of war in my soul; the spiritual warfare was real. This was going to be the biggest trial yet, with my life hanging in the balances while I was only in the baby stages of my relationship with the Lord. I wanted so much for my children to witness my baptism. But Mohamed was serious about killing me. I was afraid of him and felt that I did not know either him or what he was capable of doing anymore.

I couldn't help wondering whether baptism was worth dying for. I remember sitting at my dining-room table contemplating all this, with doubts circulating through my mind.

What if God is not really real?

Can I afford to take such a risk on my life?

How can I know for sure whether or not God is real?

Then I suddenly felt enlightened. It was as though I heard a still, quiet, but clear voice saying, "If you don't trust Him to the end, you will never know, will you?"

I realized that all too often I had pulled out of a trial before I got to see the end result, never having the patience to wait and see whether or not God would come through. I believe this was one of the contributing factors that led me away from Christ and the church. I had never known Jesus as a personal friend and had never learned to trust Him or give Him the control over my life. Now what would be the outcome of this life of mistrust? I had to learn to trust, to know that God would be victorious in the end. Finally, faith took over, and I said, "If I perish I perish"—I would rather die for Christ's sake and err on the side of right than err on the side of wrong. I agreed with the apostle Paul in Philippians 1:21, "For to me to live is Christ, and to die is gain."

I devoted the week leading up to my baptism day to prayer and fasting and to seeking God's guidance and wisdom on how to handle each trial. The church was also praying, and although I experienced some trepidation, I felt an inner peace and tranquillity just knowing that God was in control.

At the Communion service the Friday night before the baptism, I testified of God's goodness to me and shared with my fellow believers my desire to have my children accompany me to church and witness my immersion into the watery grave of baptism. I felt assured as I returned home that Jesus was going to do something great for me and the children.

Details of how I imagined the happy occasion would turn out played over and over again in my mind as I made my way home. I decided to ask Mohamed one more time if he would let the children accompany me to church the next day. Apparently out of frustration from having to listen to my now repeated plea, he raised his fist and smacked me right in the face. His reaction surprised us both. He had never done anything like that before. I did not know him to be a violent person. But clearly, he was not in control of himself; a new spirit was controlling him. I recognized this, and the Lord gave me the strength to look at him with love and forgiving pity.

As I reviewed in my mind the events leading up to this moment, it was evident that the hand of God was directing me, even though for years I had left Him out of my plans and out of my life.

I was born and reared in a Seventh-day Adventist home, one of eight children—four boys and four girls—that kept my parents busy. Home in the beautiful countryside of Gloucester, England, was warm, loving, and comfortable. Ours was a typical, devout Christian family; religion was a major part of our lives, and we children went through the rituals of regular church attendance, church participation, and baptism. I was baptized at the age of thirteen, along with some of my church friends. I didn't give it much thought; it was the natural thing to do as part of my Christian upbringing.

Leaving home some years later at the age of seventeen to attend nursing school in Surrey, near London, I experienced a new freedom that I was unaccustomed to. There was no one there to tell me what to do; I could make my own decisions. I could go where I wanted to go, wear what I wanted to wear, choose my own friends, do what I wanted to do, and have a "good" time. I was not careful in choosing my friends. Life revolved around one party or another, one dance or another. My whole emphasis was on having fun, fun, and more fun, and before I knew it, I was drinking, partying, and smoking too.

There wasn't much time for religion; life was too exciting. I reasoned that because I was reared in a Christian home, everything was going to be all right. I could live on the edge because I was in control; I knew just how

10

far to go without being hurt, I reasoned. I imagined that I would be safe from the pitfalls that others had fallen into. After all, my family was constantly praying for me, and God would surely answer their prayers if not mine.

It was during this time that I met Mohamed, one of the percussionists in my brother's band. As I attended the group's rehearsal one night, there he was—tall and handsome with those alluring dark eyes, nice, wavy black hair, and that captivating and mysterious Arab look. It was love at first sight. When our eyes met, I could feel the electricity between us.

Mohamed asked me out the same week. He was really easy to talk to. It didn't take long for him to tell me that I would be his wife. He was the man of my dreams, and I was madly in love. The feelings of love and passion enveloped me as I found myself totally immersed in the warmth of the relationship. It was hard to get thoughts of him out of my mind even as I struggled to continue nursing school. As our friendship grew, I remember communicating with God only to let Him know that Mohamed was the man I wanted and that I was determined to have him no matter what happened. I guess I was like Samson, whose attraction to Delilah clouded all rational thoughts. Little did I know at the time that I was to learn a very hard lesson on the utter irresponsibility of leaving God out of my plans.

During our courtship, Mohamed and I talked about many things, but never once did the subject of religion come up. I was only nineteen years old, and I became pregnant very early in our relationship. I tried desperately to return to church, thinking I really needed the Lord to forgive me and help me. I could no longer continue in the nurses training program, even though I had only six months to go.

I left Surrey and returned to my hometown in Gloucester, where my family and Mohamed lived. I was taken off the membership list at my church. They would not allow me to sing with my church group or take part in anything. That really hurt. I felt so rejected. I felt so embarrassed and ashamed of my enlarging abdomen. There were also feelings of guilt that I had to deal with because I had disappointed my family, church, and friends.

Looking back, I can now understand the reason for this kind of response toward teen pregnancy in the church. It's good to know that God is willing to wink at our times of ignorance (Acts 17:30). Teen pregnancy is a common occurrence in our churches, but many choose abortion nowadays to keep their secret from being revealed, and they can keep up an appearance of a "good Christian character." Others who choose to come forth with their child are often ridiculed and rejected and even ostracized by some church members.

Our churches need to educate their young members on sexual issues and spirituality. Then the adult members should be educated on how to receive and accept pregnant members who are unmarried and how to work to either encourage and keep them in the church or reach out to them if they have left the church. Sex was not a subject talked about in the church I attended, and the pregnancy rate among our teens rose each year.

My interest in the church grew very dim, and just before the birth of my son, Mohamed and I decided to move into an apartment together. Five months after my son's birth I became pregnant again, this time with twins. During this pregnancy Mohamed went to live in India for six months. His parents sent him there because they wanted him to find a Muslim wife. This was unknown to me at the time. He arrived back in time for the birth of the twins. Now we had three sons.

Three weeks after the twins were born, my parents left England to live in the United States. I missed them very much—they had been so supportive of me. Soon after that, Mohamed left again, but this time for Canada to stay with his sister for a while. I think that he was in shock at having so many children in the space of just two years.

When he left I felt so alone that I started to pray again. "What shall I do, where shall I go?" I asked God. My parents kept calling for me to come and live in the United States and make a new start. The idea sounded good. I was tired of Mohamed being such an inconsistent father, so I decided to take up my parents' offer, and I immigrated to the United States with my three sons. This gave me a sense of freedom—a new chapter to my life had begun. There was no one here who knew who I was or knew anything about my past. I was prepared to raise my sons by myself.

A New Beginning

I had told Mohamed that I needed to move on with my life. He was upset with me and started talking about being more consistent in his sons' lives. He even discussed marriage. I told him I didn't think it would work because we had a difference in religious beliefs. Once again he started to tug away at my heart, and six weeks after I had immigrated, he came to the United States. No sooner had he arrived than we started making plans for a wedding—much to the distress of our parents.

We planned to raise the boys with a Christian/Islamic perspective, and when they were old enough to choose, we would allow them to choose between the two religions. These were hurried plans, plans made without consulting the Lord, and so on July 28, 1982, we were married by a justice of the peace, and we later had a Muslim wedding at the local mosque. I had wished for a Christian blessing but just never got around to doing it.

Looking back, I wonder how God could have blessed that which He had forbidden. God has said we must not be unequally yoked with unbelievers (2 Corinthians 6:14). Even if you do have children together, that does not give you the right to try to correct things that God has already forbidden. Sex outside of marriage is fornication. To try to atone for that sin by getting married to an unbeliever only makes matters worse. That is certainly what happened in my case.

Two wrongs don't make a right, and this was the lesson I had to learn. Even if you make a mistake and conceive a child, that doesn't mean that you have to marry your partner. My advice would be to not make the mistake I made, even if the person is a church member. Consider carefully whether the person you are involved with will make a good husband. Do not rush into a marriage that you will regret.

To church members who know a woman or man in this situation—just know that they need to feel genuine love and acceptance from you. To the individuals I would say that you may be taken off the church record books but don't be angry or resentful. Rather, take time to reevaluate your walk with the Lord. Recommit yourself to walking with God—chances are good that the church will eventually welcome you back. People do not always act correctly in church, but the wheat and the tares must grow together until the time of harvest. As you make your come-back with the Lord, you will grow to love those who had nasty things to say about you.

However great the consequences for the sins we commit, greater still is the victory over any kind of sin. God can help you to accept your situation and face the consequences. Even though we crucify Christ all over again when we fall, He comes back to us and gives us encouragement and power to deal with the consequences that we have brought on our-selves. That's why Jesus died the death we were so deserving of. So, when we fall, let us humble ourselves, repent, ask for forgiveness, and seek God's will once again.

Mohamed was a very silent type of person. It soon became apparent to me how little I knew about the man I had married and how little he knew about me. Our backgrounds were a complete mystery to each other. One of the few details I knew about him was that he had always wanted to have lots of children. When our children were born, he was there for each birth and was the first to hold them. I loved him even more when I'd watch him take each child fresh from the womb over to the window in the birthing room and whisper something in the baby's ear. It seemed like a cute and loving thing to do. I didn't know that he was giving them the initial call to Islam by repeating the Muslim call to prayer, which meant that the baby became a Muslim from that point on.

Mohamed and I hardly ever argued—everything seemed wonderful. After some years in the United States we had two more children, girls this time. Mohamed was firm with the boys, but the girls brought out the tenderness in him.

In the early years of our marriage, neither Mohamed nor I remained very committed to our religious upbringing. We still held to the idea that we would teach both of our religions to our children so that they would have a basis to make a choice when they became adults; we made our-selves believe that was what would work best.

By the time all the children were born, my church attendance was spo-radic and my decision to teach the children about Christianity was little more than a good intention. Mohamed, however, did begin to teach the boys the Arabic alphabet while they were still very young. As the years went by, he added Arabic prayers and some teachings about Islam to their instruction. The boys were soon praying in Arabic. The influence of Islam was subtly creeping into our home and into our lives. I was so far from God that I did not recognize the power that was in control of my home.

At times I felt the prompting of the Holy Spirit urging me to let Christ enter my life, but somehow I felt that if I pursued that course, it would cause problems in our home. I wanted so much to preserve the peaceful atmosphere. A few times I did tell Mohamed that I wanted to attend church and take the children along with me, but he always replied, "If you do, you will never see them again." Whenever he said that, I felt a little fearful, but he would just laugh it off as if he was only joking. Beyond the jovial exterior, however, I sensed something much more serious.

About a year after the birth of our second daughter, I once again felt the Holy Spirit pleading with me to return to the Lord. This time, however, was very different from all the other times. There was a sense of urgency accompanied by a very ominous feeling and fear of death. I wondered what would happen if I died and lost my soul. What would happen to the children, especially since they had no knowledge of Christ? I had neglected to teach them about the One who loved them infinitely more than I ever could. I had failed in this most important responsibility of parenthood. I knew I needed to do something fast. It was a real emergency that I reestablish my relationship with Christ. This time I was not concerned about the effects on my marriage. Returning to the Lord was now a priority.

How could I have denied my children the experience of knowing God that I had enjoyed so much when I was a child? As I felt the intense longing for Christ and for peace of mind, it seemed I could still hear the voice of my kindergarten Sabbath School teacher as she related the thrilling stories of Jesus. In my mind's eye, I could see as clearly as on the days I sat in those tiny seats, the lovely pictures on the felt board. I began to wish for the same experiences for my children, the same joy that I had of being raised in a Christian home.

Meanwhile, Mohamed was focusing more intensely on teaching the children about Islam. I could tell that the children were unhappy as they studied. I looked into their little eyes; there was no joy there. The studies were very stressful for them. They did not understand the language; they did not know what the prayers meant. And Mohamed often lost his patience and would slap them whenever they made a mistake in the memorization of the prayers.

The sight of their sad, tear-stained faces day after day as they were forced to sit for long periods and learn sections of prayer was almost more than I could bear. I wanted so much to do something, but I did not know what to do. Should I take the children and leave home? But where would I go? What would Mohamed do to me? I was becoming more and more unhappy in my marriage. I would often ask myself, Is this it? Is this what marriage is all about?

There was a dark, heavy cloud over my union with Mohamed. I was experiencing the reality of a wrong choice in a marriage partner. What I thought was fine gold was really tarnished brass. The passion, the lust was gone, and I was left empty to bear my lot.

We had nothing in common other than the children. We couldn't communicate well with each other. My sad life was little more than drudgery, yet my Christian upbringing wouldn't allow me to leave my husband. I knew marriage was for a lifetime, so I decided to do the best I could with the situation. But I needed help to bear the load, and I had abandoned the only help I had, which was Christ.

The struggles I was going through affected me physically, mentally, and spiritually. I suffered from heart palpitations, and most of the time I felt weak and exhausted. The stress was having a devastating effect on me. I was constantly afraid of dying and leaving my children without the sure anchor that could only be found in Jesus. I found myself crying out in my distress, "Oh, Jesus, if You are real and if You are merciful, help me! I don't know where to turn for help." In my heart I knew that if there was an answer to my problems, it could only be found in Jesus. But I was so far from Him, I wondered whether He would hear and answer my prayers.

16

chapter 2

Toward the Light

I had just finished the night shift and was heading home. The sun was bright orange, and the reflection on my car was so powerful that it appeared to me that the car was on fire. As irrational as that may seem, it caused a chilling fear to fill my heart, and I almost lost control of the car. Thoughts of death troubled me constantly, and fear was my ever-present companion.

One night, as I was lying in bed, it seemed I could hear a voice in my mind saying, "Esmie, you are not dying a physical death; you are dying spiritually." It startled me! I began to wonder whether I was losing my mind. I could not shake the reality of what I had experienced. It was different—compelling, yet gentle! I pondered the words and realized that there was a lot of truth to them. But I had no idea what I could do about my seemingly hopeless situation.

Two nights later, I dreamed that I encountered my already-deceased father in a room flooded with light. He was eating bread, and I begged him to share it with me. Instead of sharing, he pointed toward an arched window. As I looked out the window and into the blue sky, I saw the form of Jesus beckoning me to come to Him. I wanted to have some of the delicious bread, but my father shook his head, indicating that I had to receive my own from Jesus. I knew then that Christ was calling me out of spiritual darkness into His light and that it was an urgent call.

Some time later, I started reading a booklet called *Steps to Christ*, which my mother had put in my suitcase when I first left home. The book captivated me and held me spellbound until I completed it. It was exactly what I needed. Each word, each sentence, each paragraph seemed to be written just for me. I was amazed at how much God knew of the details of my life and could inspire the author to write a book to meet my needs. I wondered, *Who is this God who knows me so intimately?* My friend and co-worker Olga Smith suggested that I should read *The Desire of Ages* by the same author. This book told the story of Jesus. As I read it, my heart began to melt. The light had begun to shine, and I was eager for more. It seemed as if I could not get enough spiritually uplifting reading material. I didn't enjoy reading before, but now I prayed for wisdom, and the Lord gave me the desire to read and to know more about Him.

The more I read, the more I craved spiritual things, and the tugging at my heartstrings became very real. I felt a power drawing me back to Christ and to the church. I developed an intense hunger for spiritual things. As the weeks went by, I felt a deep longing to recapture the spiritual experiences of my childhood and youth. I wanted to sit in the congregation and sing. I wanted to sing those old hymns again: *Blessed Assurance, Jesus Is Mine; Redeemed, How I Love to Proclaim It.* I wanted to sing so much, it was almost overwhelming. I recognized that God was leading me back to Him. Now, I could finally say "Yes, Lord."

As I sang the old songs I had learned as a child, I began to listen to my own voice singing and felt that the Lord was leading me through their simple messages. I asked for a special anointing on my voice so I could sing to the honor and glory of God. God did not respond positively to that request until many years later, after I had endured many trials and reached the point where I was willing to deny self.

As I began to seek Him for daily guidance, my faith grew stronger. God made it clear to me through His promises that I did not have to run away with my children but that He would deliver my children and me from Islam. Still some big questions loomed in my mind, not the least of which were, "How could I tell Mohamed what was happening inside of me? How could I go to church? There were periods of doubt because I wanted to please my husband and I could see that my actions troubled him. But I did not want to ignore the Holy Spirit's prompting. I decided to step out in faith and begin attending church alone.

One Wednesday night in the winter of 1987, I made up my mind to attend the Faith Seventh-day Adventist Church in Hartford, Connecticut. As I approached the doors, I felt like the prodigal son returning to a loving father. Even though the members did not know me, they were warm and loving, and I felt comfortable and at home among them. They sang the words to that prayer-meeting favorite *Sweet Hour of Prayer*, and I felt a calm, warm feeling of home.

The study that night was on the book of Revelation. I heard truths that night that I had not heard before. I thought that I knew everything, having been reared in the Adventist Church. But that night the Bible came alive. A peace and an inner strength began to develop inside me. My life was changing rapidly. God was truly alive! He was real! I could feel His tender leading in my life. His words were truth, and my heart was convinced.

The Bible was life to me. Through its pages, I could hear God speaking to me and telling me, "This is the way; walk ye in it." I spent many days walking and talking with Him, reasoning with Him, and telling Him about all my fears. I could sense that there was a great battle at hand, and I needed all the strength that I could muster to face it.

I wanted to join the church choir and was told that I should consider enrolling in the baptismal classes and being rebaptized first. I felt I needed to be rebaptized because I had strayed so far away from God, doing anything and everything I felt like doing for so many years. I wanted to make a statement to the world that I was now choosing a better course. I was guided through the Amazing Facts Bible study course, and the Lord made clear His will that I dedicate my life anew to Him.

Soon I had completed the baptismal lessons and was ready to be baptized. I wanted so much for the children to witness this occasion. In my judgment, I had been a good mother, only I didn't teach my children about Jesus. I was willing to make amends because now that I was a Christian I knew that I was responsible also for their spiritual upbringing. Once I decided to make Christianity a part of my life, I had attempted to witness to Mohamed about Jesus Christ, but he demanded that I never again suggest that Jesus was Lord and Savior. To Mohamed, Jesus was just a prophet.

chapter 3

What a Day!

The sheer beauty of this new day—the Sabbath of the Lord—and the chills running up and down my spine brought me back to reality. As the thoughts raced through my mind, I concluded that I had made the right decision. Today was the day I had planned to be baptized. I wondered why the week had been so terrible. As I opened the Word of God, the Holy Spirit spoke to me in the book of Luke, chapter 12, verses 50, 51. " 'But I have a baptism to be baptized with; and how am I straitened till it be accomplished! Suppose ye that I am come to give peace on earth? I tell you, Nay; but rather division.' "

I understood this to be the voice of God explaining the difficulties I had encountered after making my decision to follow Him all the way, and I praised Him for making things plain to me. Tears of joy and gratitude spilled down my cheeks from the realization that Jesus loved me so much that He protected me in my sinful state while I was so far away from Him. He preserved me, and I was not deserving of this. I broke down in deepest sorrow for my sins and for my past life apart from Him.

Jesus showed me that this was true repentance. I told Him I could never make up for the pain that I had caused Him. All I had to give was myself, and that was all that He said He wanted. I wanted to obey Him and to do everything He commanded. I just had to please my lovely Jesus.

By this time I heard Mohamed stirring. I knew that he was awake, and fear came over me as I awaited my death. I had purposely left out clothes for the children to wear on their first trip to church. I was determined to bring them so they could witness my baptism. Mohamed knew this, but a miracle took place right before my very eyes. A peaceful calm came over Mohamed as he prepared himself for work and left without saying a word.

Once again, I praised God for His great power and protection. I quickly woke the children, led them in family worship, and started to get ready for church. Mohamed had taken the car, so we decided to walk. I put the baby in the stroller, and the other four children walked by my side. With a heart full of gratitude to God for answering my prayer in such a miraculous way, my steps were lightened, and the three-mile walk to church seemed a small price to pay in return.

As we arrived, the members cheerfully greeted us; they were happy to see the children. The children were well-behaved. Even though they were not accustomed to sitting in a church service, they sat quietly and absorbed it all. The church members were very helpful with the children. My sister, who had started attending church as a result of the changes she had seen in my life, helped out as well. The Lord blessed, and the service was beautiful.

After the baptism, the pastor made an appeal for others to join the baptismal class and prepare for a future baptism. I was pleasantly surprised to see Javid, my oldest son, who was only eight years old at the time, stand to his feet with his hands raised and tears streaming down his face, indicating that he wanted to be baptized.

Soon afterward, Javid enrolled in the baptismal class, but when Mohamed learned about this, he told Javid never to call him father again. It was very difficult for my son at such a tender age to hear such harsh words from his father. Except for the Arabic lessons, he had always enjoyed his father's company and cherished the times the family spent together. He found it very difficult to endure, but he prayed to God and was comforted through His Word.

What a Day!

I gave Javid a Bible and told him to go away by himself and talk to God. When he came back, he read 1 Peter 1:7 to me and said, "Mom, I may not have an earthly father, but I do have a heavenly Father."

My heart was thrilled to hear this. Javid completed his studies, stood for Christ, and was baptised

One morning as we were having worship, Adam, one of the twins, told me about a strange dream that he had had the night before. In his dream, someone had knocked on the door of our apartment while I was at work. His father was in the living room. He opened the door. There in the doorway stood a tall figure, and a brilliant light shone into and through the apartment. My three sons looked into the light, and it did not hurt them; but as their father looked into the light, it blinded him.

Immediately, I knew that this dream was from the Holy Spirit. The light of heaven truly had begun to shine into our home, and my children and I were receiving that light. But Mohamed had refused to receive it.

Javid's decision to be baptized set off another round of affliction for the entire family. Mohamed became physically abusive toward me; he stopped buying food for the family and kept the car from me. However, whenever the children and I prayed, there would inevitably be a knock on the door and family and church members bringing just the right necessities for us.

Our faith was growing stronger and stronger as we witnessed the Lord's direct intervention in our lives from day to day. We were dedicated to serving Him all the days of our lives, and He rewarded our faith with manifold blessings.

The Holy Spirit had done for my children what I could never have done for them. I could never undo the teaching and training they had undergone in our home. But the Holy Spirit was making the truth very clear to them.

chapter 4

The Call to Go

As my newfound joy in Christ became more and more a part of my life, Mohamed grew very indifferent toward me. Sometimes he acted as if I did not exist. He spent a lot of time at the mosque with his Saudi friends. I wanted a better relationship with my husband, not only for me but for the children.

Mohamed made several attempts to take the children away from me. One time, he planned to take them to Canada, and from there to Saudi Arabia. But I insisted on going along on the trip. I later learned that that was one of his attempts to take them away.

After some time, I noticed that he was becoming more considerate and understanding. He was more caring toward us, buying us food, and even dropping us off at church and picking us up after services. I was beginning to think that the Holy Spirit was finally finding a way to his heart. Actually, he was planning to take the family to live in Saudi Arabia. He started to talk about going to Saudi Arabia and about the great job opportunities there. I didn't care much for the idea, but he decided that he would go on ahead and look for a job. One of his Saudi friends was from a wealthy family that owned businesses. They promised to set him up. So the children and I remained in the United States.

About two months after he left, he sent for us to come, but I was not prepared to leave, and I needed to hear from God. So I told him that we were not ready to come yet and that I wasn't sure we ever would be. This made him very angry, because I was spoiling his plans.

Life was very difficult for the children and me. He stopped supporting us; this was his way of forcing us to be where he was. We had no food and no money. Eventually, we were evicted from our spacious condominium, and a church family took us into their basement apartment.

Mohamed returned to the United States in order to convince me to go. He was angry that he had to come all the way back to convince me. He stayed at the mosque because, of course, we had no home. He told me that all the plans for us to go to Saudi Arabia had been made. A house and a job were waiting.

I desperately needed to hear from God. I feverishly studied the Word of God for any indication of which way the Lord was leading. I prayed and fasted. Little by little, God began to reveal His will and His directions for us. I felt sure that God wanted us to go with Mohamed to Saudi Arabia. It was not what I wanted, but it seemed clear to me that it was God's will and that He had a purpose for us there.

God's leading was clear and distinct. He had a purpose for us, His children, to enter into an area of darkness to share the light of the gospel. *The Adventist Home*, page 488, seemed to be written in answer to my prayers. It said the following:

> God calls for Christian families to go into communities that are in darkness and error, and work wisely and perseveringly for the Master. To answer this call requires self-sacrifice. While many are waiting to have every obstacle removed, souls are dying without hope and without God in the world. Many, very many, for the sake of worldly advantage, for the sake of acquiring scientific knowledge, will venture into pestilential regions and endure hardship and privation. Where are those who are willing to do this for the sake of telling others of the Saviour? Where are the men and women who will move into re-

gions that are in need of the gospel, that they may point those in darkness to the Redeemer?

If families would locate in the dark places of the earth, places where the people are enshrouded in spiritual gloom, and let the light of Christ's life shine out through them, a great work might be accomplished. Let them begin their work in a quiet, unobtrusive way, not drawing on the funds of the conference until the interest becomes so extensive that they cannot manage it without ministerial help.

Although I felt that the call to Saudi Arabia was real, I continued praying and fasting. During the weeks that ensued, every prayer, every sermon, every impression seemed to be pointing me in that direction. I realized that as a Christian wife and mother, my duty toward my family was very important. I also knew that the gospel had to be preached in all the world. I began to feel that I had been chosen by God to do the wonderful work of carrying the good news of the gospel to Saudi Arabia while fulfilling my duty to my husband and children. I just knew that there would be people there anxiously waiting to hear about the Lord.

My excitement was tempered with some fear because I didn't know what to expect. Fear was the only excuse I could come up with as a reason not to go, and I knew God was not the author of fear. I was excited, knowing that I was about to embark on a great witness for the Lord.

During this time I was working selling religious and health books, and the Lord had blessed me with a brand-new car. I wondered what I would do with the car. I was still making payments. But the Lord worked everything out, and a church member bought the car from me. Everything was coming together. My church family gave us a wonderful farewell, and I received many cards and gifts. Finally all the farewells were said, and we were on our way, first to spend some time with my mother and other family members in England and then on to Saudi Arabia.

My family in England was very concerned about us going, but when they heard my testimony of God's leading and saw my determination to do the Lord's will, they resigned themselves to the fact that there was little they could do to dissuade me.

We spent three months in England. During this time I kept building on my relationship with Jesus. I kept reading and getting to know Him better. I was comforted by reading about the apostle Paul who had spent three years in Saudi Arabia. I realized that I wasn't the only one who had to endure isolation in order to do God's will.

On the night before we left England, I was impressed to wear a Muslim outfit. I did not question God on this , I just obeyed. I owned many books, and as I was packing I prayed over them and discreetly placed them into my suitcases. I wanted to have a lot of material to read to fill up any lonely moments so far away from family and friends, and I wanted to get to know Jesus even more. So I tore off the covers from the hardback books and wrapped them in sweaters and towels so that everything would feel soft and be well hidden. Mohamed had warned me not to bring any Christian books because they would be searched out and confiscated, and our lives would be put in jeopardy. We could even be imprisoned if we were caught with any Christian material.

chapter 5

To Places Unknown

As we checked our luggage at Heathrow airport in London, I noticed that the suitcases were not bulging as much as they were when I packed them. But I dismissed any thought that anything was amiss. I just figured that the clothing and my books had settled in place. I had packed many books in the suitcases; however, some of my most treasured religious books—*Steps to Christ, Counsels on Diets and Foods, The Desire of Ages, The Adventist Home,* as well as my Sabbath School lesson quarterly and some other Christian literature—were in my hand luggage along with a Walkman, some music tapes, and a few sermons on tape.

During the entire flight, I was quiet and in deep communion with my God as I contemplated the awesome responsibility resting on me to take the gospel truths to this dark country. As we flew over Syria, the children were fascinated by the beautiful city lights, but by now I was thinking of what could happen if the books that I had packed were discovered. I prayed all the more, for now my greatest concern was for my books to get through customs.

We landed at Dharan Airport in Saudi Arabia at midnight, July

24, 1989. It was ninety degrees and very humid. As we walked into customs, I prayed, "Lord, point me to the right customs official." Just then, an older man came up and directed us to the first desk. I was praying more feverishly in my mind about those books. It began to dawn on me what a dangerous thing I had done. I knew I could be prosecuted, even executed, for trying to smuggle contraband into the country.

The customs officials began searching the suitcases. As I watched with rapt attention, I could almost hear my heart pounding in my chest. To my amazement, they were not finding the books. I was happy, overjoyed. Trying hard to control my excitement, I thought, *God is performing a great miracle here*. But as the search revealed no books, I started to get a little suspicious and wondered, *Where are the books?*

Then the suitcase that contained my Bible was placed on the desk for inspection; I prayed more earnestly than ever. I stared as the customs officials dug deep and pulled out the Bible wrapped snugly in a sweater. It obviously had been hidden. They unwrapped it and started to flick through the pages. My heart was racing as fear almost overwhelmed me. I had torn off the covers of the Bible and other hardcover books, hoping that the softer feel would make them more difficult to detect. But now, my worst fears were realized.

The Holy Spirit impressed me to remain silent, not to show any emotion, and to watch for His salvation. I prayed, "Lord, Your Word is a lamp unto my feet and a light unto my path. I need Your Word. Please do not let them take it away from me." Other officials were called over, and as they approached with guns in hand, I stood trembling in a desperate attempt to maintain my composure. It suddenly occurred to me that my Muslim attire was my cover, and I began to praise God in my heart for impressing me to dress this way.

From outward appearances, we were a typical Muslim family. The officials spoke in their language and kept looking at us as they flicked through the pages of the Bible. They turned to a very nervous Mohamed and asked, "Are you Muslim?"

"Yes, of course," he said.

"Then let me see your ID," they demanded.

Mohamed handed over the document. His name and his long beard, typical of most Muslim men, conveyed to them his Muslim background. They did not speak to me because female to male contact in Saudi Arabia is not socially acceptable, especially in the presence of the husband. They were silent for what seemed like an eternity wrapped up in a few minutes. Suddenly, they burst out into laughter saying, "You are Muslims. Go. We will search no more suitcases because we trust you." Praises were on my lips and hallelujahs in my heart. What a great God we serve!

My personal hand luggage with books that would have identified me with Christianity was not inspected. They put my Bible back into the suitcase, closed it, and put blue stickers on the rest of the luggage indicating that they had been inspected, even though they had not. God had intervened as He always does. I had witnessed the first of many miracles God was going to perform for me in Saudi Arabia. There was no reason for the officials to return my Bible, other than the working of a loving God on my behalf. Truly God was with me; I felt His assurance and His comfort as I walked boldly through customs, out the door, and on my way to do my Father's business.

Sammy, Mohamed's sponsor, met us at the airport with his servants. He was genuinely glad to see us. I could see it on his face as he made his approach toward us. Sammy and Mohamed greeted each other with hugs, kisses, and a look of relief on their faces.

"You made it, then," Sammy said with a grin.

I knew exactly what that meant. The fact that the children and I were in Saudi Arabia meant that Mohamed had finally won the battle over the religion issue in our home and that his family was finally back in his grip.

The servants took our luggage, and we piled into the car and started off for the city of Damman where we were to live. The city was half an hour away. To my surprise, we pulled into a hotel parking lot. Mohamed had told me that there was a house waiting for us. Later that night, I also found out that Mohamed had no job. Here we were in the Middle East with no source of income and no place to live.

I began to unpack the suitcases only to find that all the books that I had packed indeed were not there. Only the ones in my hand luggage were left. I asked Mohamed if he knew what had happened to them. He looked at me and laughed, saying, "Do you really think I would be stupid enough not to check the luggage before we got here? I emptied out all your Christian books and threw them in the garbage in England."

Not only did he throw away my books, but he had discarded all the gifts and cards from my family and from my church family back in Connecticut. I was devastated and so hurt; those gifts had sentimental value, especially a very old hymnbook that belonged to my deceased father. Mother had given it to me before I left. And there was a very beautiful plaque that I treasured from the members of my prayer meeting group. The books and tapes were very dear to me. They held many memories of how the Lord had led me in the past. Everything was destroyed! I was outraged. Anger filled me; I wanted to scream at him, but I controlled myself, knowing that I was completely at the mercy of Mohamed. He could do anything to me. No one knew me in Saudi Arabia, and I would have nowhere to go. Home for me was far, far away.

I was so hurt that I began to doubt God's leading. The miracle I thought God had performed at the airport by concealing the books was only a figment of my imagination. Mohamed had already thrown away the books, even before we left England. Clouds of doubt enveloped me. What if I had been mistaken? Did God really want me to come to this place? Or did I make it all up? Questions crowded my thinking, and the weight of the trials I was facing seemed too heavy to bear.

But I could not give up on God now. I was so far away from the people and the places I loved. My only link to them was through the Holy Spirit. So I prayed and asked God for endurance and faith to face the days ahead. I asked Him to increase my trust in Him. This was my first test, and I felt that I needed to pass it quickly and well. Somehow, I sensed that there would be greater trials yet to come. So I pulled myself together by His grace and accepted the loss of my precious belongings.

I prayed that my books would somehow find their way into the hands of someone who would read the books and listen to the tapes and find some of the joy and comfort I had found in them. As I resigned myself to the loss, I comforted myself by telling the Lord that I expected to see some person or persons in His kingdom who would have found Christ through those discarded books. And I still had several other great books that Mohamed had not found. I kept those with me always.

chapter 6

A Faithful Witness

Because we had arrived at night, my first real glimpse of the country did not come until the next morning. As I peered through the window, everything looked brown and blighted. There was hardly any greenery. The few trees and patches of grass that were there were carefully grown by fertilizers and irrigation. Everywhere seemed colorless. The heat was stifling, and the smell of sewage permeated the air. The streets were practically empty during the day because of the heat. This just added to my sense of loss. I felt very lonely, very isolated.

Mohamed left for Sammy's office later that morning. Sammy was one of the brothers Mohamed had met in Connecticut. He had completed his studies and returned to his country. He was from a wealthy background, and he had promised to set Mohamed up with a job at one of his businesses. While Mohamed was gone, I gathered the children for family worship. Then I called my family in England and the United States to let them know that we had arrived safely. I shared with them my concern regarding the facts that Saturday was considered the first day of the week in Saudi Arabia, that my children would be expected to attend school on the Sabbath, and that weekends were Thursday and Friday, with Friday being the holy day.

33

Beyond the Veil of Darkness

I wondered what kind of difficulties lurked in our future. I didn't want the children breaking the Sabbath. I prayed, "Lord, please don't let my children ever have to attend school on the Sabbath." I did not know how He was going to answer that prayer, but I just believed that He would.

Then I began to wonder where we could worship God on the Sabbath. It seemed impossible to keep the Sabbath holy without going to church. My sister assured me that God would accept our worship even if it was not in a church by saying that the Sabbath is written on the heart and that under the circumstances it could be kept without going to church. I was to learn quickly that the Sabbath was to be kept in our hearts as a result of a spiritual union with God.

In time, the conversation with my sister played over and over again in my head, which led me to the realization that there are many reasons why people attend church. Some do so out of guilt, from force of habit, or as part of the weekly routine. But God tells us that we should worship Him in spirit and in truth. This was comforting and reassuring to me; for the first time, I was going to experience this type of worship. I said, "Lord, it's just You and me now. I have no friends to call upon, no one to talk to, no one to advise me, no one to encourage me except You, Lord."

When I finally arrived at this conclusion in my discussion with the Lord, I felt assured that He would accept our worship and remove the "guilt" of not attending a church. Everything I needed from this point onward had to come directly from God.

When Mohamed returned home from Sammy's office that first day, he told us to get ready to go to the marketplace. I welcomed the chance to escape my feeling of depression and thought that the outing would lift my spirits. We were chauffeured to the marketplace, where we got out and started to walk around examining the merchandise. Suddenly, I felt I was the center of attention. All eyes were upon me, looking at me in disgust. I felt naked as though I was walking around exposed. Then it dawned on me that the only faces I could see were the faces of men. The women were covered with a strange, black, thin material from head to toe. Their faces were covered too, and I could not tell if they, too, were looking at me.

A Faithful Witness

My husband took me to a stall that sold beautiful dresses. I wondered if he was going to buy me a beautiful, new dress. But that thought was short-lived. Instead, he picked out one of the black outfits similar to the ones I had observed the women wearing, along with a black scarf for my head. As he paid for them, he instructed me to wear them whenever I left the hotel or thought to go outside of our home.

The black outfit is called an abaya. In fact, it has many other names, depending on what part of the Middle East you are from. I asked, "Why black?" It was explained to me that black is considered an ugly color, so the women wear this ugly, loose, shapeless cover so as to prevent the men from falling into temptation. If the men were to look on the woman and her shape, form, and beauty, they would sin because they would commit adultery.

This was deep to say the least. Today we see Christian women dressed in hardly any clothes. Our backs are exposed, thighs are showing, our breasts are exposed in tight and low cut garments. I say we can learn a lot from other religions and their conduct. In Islamic countries women are modest, and I appreciated that. Some may think dress reform to be extreme, but dress is an important part of who we are, and Whose we are. Some of us need to take a second look at ourselves and do some serious reevaluation. We must look for truth in every circumstance and use it to enhance our faith.

I began to practice taking the good out of every bad situation. I was glad to have an abaya especially in the mornings when I needed to get something for breakfast from the corner store before the children awoke. I would just throw on that black cover and take off speedily to the store. Besides, I was always one for wearing unusual clothes as a child.

There were so many adjustments that I had to make. I felt very restricted in what I was allowed to do. The realization that my life was not going to be the same as long as I remained in this country struck me forcibly. Once again, I prayed that God would help me to adjust quickly to the customs of the land, its culture, and its people.

That evening, we were invited to Sammy's home. When we arrived, the first thing I noticed was that the house had four entrances, two for the men and two for the women. Mohamed and the boys entered through one door, and the girls and I went through another. As soon as we were inside, Mona, Sammy's wife, greeted us warmly. She had a lovely smile and told me that she had heard a lot about me and was happy to have me in her home. Also invited that evening was Zainup, an American woman. She and her husband, a Syrian, had met as college students in North Dakota. They had three children, and she was from a Christian background, but now she was a devout Muslim.

I felt fairly comfortable with the women. After we greeted each other, I removed my covering, for there were only women on this side of their large home. We sat down together on Mona's beautiful Persian rug and began to talk. The ladies asked me questions about my religious faith, and I was able to share with them some of my experiences with God. I was aware of their belief that Jesus was merely a prophet and not the Son of God, so out of respect for what they believed, I referred to Jesus as God often using the name Allah when referring to God. I never used the name of Jesus as a point of reference unless they brought up His name in a form of question. I was able to witness about who Jesus was to me. They seemed to appreciate my willingness to answer their questions. I felt they respected me and what I believed.

They asked many more questions, and I was happy to answer them, convinced that this was the Lord's way of using me to witness to them. The Lord gave me wisdom; I was careful not to force my own religious beliefs on them but to keep myself under the control of the Holy Spirit while answering their questions. In this way, I knew that the Holy Spirit could use me to convey whatever message He wanted them to know at this time.

As we continued to talk, the servants served us a very attractive meal consisting of salad, chicken, rice, potatoes, and vegetables. We all sat cross-legged on the floor and ate out of the same huge tray. I was careful to use only my right hand to eat with. According to the local culture and custom and especially the Hadith, which are books filled with the living habits and practices of the prophet Mohammed, to eat with the left hand is very offensive. Also, one must sit correctly when eating and sleep only in certain positions. The list goes on and on, but as long as you follow the way prophet Mohammed conducted himself, you cannot go wrong. His ways and habits are to be duplicated in every good Muslim's life.

It did not escape Mona's notice that I was not partaking of the flesh foods or the strong black coffee placed in front of me. She inquired why I was not having any of the chicken. Here was another opportunity for me to be a witness, I thought. The Holy Spirit immediately impressed me that even though it would be difficult to talk about Jesus in countries such as Saudi Arabia, He could use the powerful health message as an entering wedge to lead others to Christ.

I needed to be careful not to offend. I started out by telling them that "our body belongs to Allah because He created us and that we should serve Him and give Him our very best. He deserves that from us." The words flowed freely from my lips. "When Allah shows us a better way and we understand it, we are obligated to abide by it through the power of Allah. It is right to care for our bodies," I said, "by eating those things that are nourishing and healthy. By so doing, we are maintaining His dwelling place. Our body is the temple of Allah. When we care for our body by not putting in anything that is stimulating, that disturbs the digestive system, or that causes disease and ailments, we can then expect to receive the benefit of a sound mind, one that is able to discern more clearly, to commune with God on a higher spiritual level, and to withstand temptations. Therefore, the mind is being strengthened."

I had said a lot. Mona looked at me with amazement. She had never heard anything like it before and was obviously deeply impressed.

"Yes," she said, "it makes sense." She then expressed her love for Allah and her resolve to have a healthier body that would stimulate a healthy mind for her to pray and have a greater understanding of Allah. This was a wonderful beginning, because with a healthier mind, one is more susceptible to truth.

After dinner, I spoke with Zainup for a while. She seemed rather timid and spoke with a heavy Arabic accent, even though she was American. Not knowing her background, one would assume that she was an Arab learning to speak English. But occasionally her American accent would come through.

Beyond the Veil of Darkness

How sad, I thought. Here was a woman who had lost her identity. An English-speaking woman from North Dakota speaking with an Arabic accent; she had only been in Saudi Arabia for two months! Her identity was deeply merged into that of her husband; she had no sense of self-worth, and she did not appear to be happy. My heart went out to her. I could see that she was happy to speak with me, because I had also come from the same culture as she had and we were able to relate and identify more readily. I felt a deep concern for this woman and her children for some reason, and I lifted her up to God in silent prayer.

Before long, however, my husband sent a message by way of the servants that he was ready to leave. The servant brought my black cover, and I thanked Mona for a lovely evening. I promised Zainup that we would spend some time getting to know each other, I bade them all Assalaamu Alaikum (peace), and left with Mohamed and the children.

That night, I praised God for the health message and for the marvelous opportunity He had given me to be His witness. I prayed for Zainup and Mona that the seeds of righteousness and truth the Holy Spirit had led me to sow would take root in the soil of their hearts.

chapter 7

The First
Sabbath

Dinner at Mona and Sammy's house was an interesting experience. I really enjoyed getting to know the women and, most of all, getting a chance to do what I was sure the Lord had led me so far from home to do—to witness for Him. Back at the hotel the next day, I busied myself with chores to keep my mind off my circumstances.

Every day, Mohamed went to Sammy's office building and spent most of the day there. He spent little time with the children and me. It was not always easy finding something to fill the hours I spent alone or with just the children. I decided to do the laundry. I gathered up all the soiled clothes and washed them by hand. I tried to focus on heavenly things, but it was a mental struggle. My entire world was confined to that little room.

On our first Friday, we were to experience the local holy day for the first time. Mohamed woke the children at 3:30 a.m. and took off to the beach with them. He did not invite me to go along, so I had no choice but to spend the day alone in a strange country.

When they left, I felt so alone; an awful fear engulfed me. I must have been half-asleep when I began to sense that someone had come into the room. But when I turned to see who it was, no one was there. Everything around me looked dark and scary. Suddenly, I felt pinned to the bed as a sensation similar to an electrical current ran through my listless body. I couldn't breathe. I felt as if the forces of evil were overpowering me. Undoubtedly, an evil spirit was contending for my very life.

I cried out to the Lord and asked Jesus to rebuke Satan. Gradually, the heaviness in the atmosphere began to lighten. I sat up and started to pray. I knew that the spiritual battle for my life was real, and I knew that I had to keep praying for strength to withstand the evil forces. I recognized the importance of keeping in constant communion with God, of maintaining a simple diet, and of reading and studying His Word.

I spent the day alone. I ordered up breakfast of toast, orange juice, and cereal. Then I proceeded to unpack some of the suitcases, and the time of silence allowed me to think and meditate on the Lord. I wondered what the future held and how long I would be here. I felt very concerned for my children's future.

The next day was our first Sabbath in Saudi Arabia. We missed home so much. I was sad, and I missed the fellowship with other Sabbath-keeping Christians. We longed for the company of other members of God's family! However, we spent the day worshiping and praying while Mohamed was at work. By now he had started to work in Sammy's office building.

I'm glad that this first Sabbath was not an indication of what other Sabbaths were going to be like. In time, the Lord showed us how to keep the Sabbath in spirit and in truth, as my sister had directed me to do. She shared with me that the Sabbath is a spiritual communion with God, a spiritual rest in mind and body. It is not so much the place of worship that matters, for it is not always convenient to worship God in a building. In time, the guilt was removed, and our Sabbaths were spent worshiping God the best way we knew how, but always with the confidence that He loved us and accepted our worship.

chapter 8

A Long Way From Home

After ten days at the hotel, we moved to an apartment. It was huge—big enough to divide into two sections for male and female entertainment and dinner parties. We had no furniture, and so Sammy loaned us some money to get the most important things we needed. We bought a stove and refrigerator. Later we bought a washing machine. Cushions placed around the walls of the living room served as chairs, and we bought mattresses for beds.

This was our home. We had no telephone and no way of contacting anyone in case of an emergency. I felt extremely isolated and lonely. No one spoke my language. I rarely saw the neighbors, and I was so dependent on Mohamed. I was totally confined by my circumstances over which I had little control.

Household chores occupied most of my time. The days just seemed to drag on and on. I spent most of the days cooking, and cooking was truly a task. Peas had to be shelled, and bugs had to be picked from the rice and vegetables; but I had all day to do this. I had nothing else to do. I washed clothes and was a dutiful wife and mother.

Every time Mohamed was away from the house, the children and I would study, read, and spend time in prayer and worship. One of the children would be stationed at the window to watch for Mohamed. If we saw him coming, we would quickly hide the few books I had been able to carry into the country in my hand luggage. The children would take out their toys, and I would work on chores in the kitchen so things would look normal when he arrived. This was beginning to make me very nervous, but we continued anyway.

I became aware that my marriage had all but completely fallen apart. There was no intimacy. Mohamed slept apart from me to punish me for not accepting Islam. He wanted me as a mother for his children, to care for them and ensure that they were fed, clothed, and kept clean. I felt no love from him. He was cold, legalistic, and harsh toward me. He would often take the children, leaving me by myself much of the time to spend hours in solitude. I often cried and prayed and asked the Lord, "How long, oh Lord?" I pleaded with God to do something to get me out of this nightmare.

The stress in my life was increasing with every passing day. I was under great oppression—even though I spent long hours alone, I felt that I had no privacy because Mohamed involved himself in every aspect of my life in order to keep a watchful eye on me. I had to give him a report of my day, whom I spoke with and where I went; he would then double check on the story with the children to see if I was telling the truth. Mohamed told me that he had all power over me, and if I did not comply with his wishes to stop teaching the children about Jesus, he would have me escorted to the airport by officials and sent back to England without my family. This made me very careful about how I would go about our secret worship time, because I would never know when he would quiz the children about how they had spent their day. I had asked God to make me wise and to keep me two steps ahead of Mohamed. So I waited for him to quiz the children, and then when he left we would have our worship. More than likely he would not quiz them twice a day; he had too many other things on his mind. It was a risk, but the Lord was on our side.

I did not receive any letters from my family for quite some time after we arrived in Saudi Arabia, and I became increasingly concerned. I had written several letters to my mother and had even sent her my faithful tithe and offerings from the little grocery money I had occasionally received. I needed every blessing that I could get, and I knew there was no greater blessing than the blessing one receives when they are faithful in tithe and offerings. It was not like my family to not respond to my letters, especially considering the fact that I was so far away from home. My mother and I had a close relationship, and we always kept in contact with each other on a regular basis.

Mohamed became tired of my complaining about not hearing from my family. One day he handed me a letter from my mother that had been written quite some time back. It was open, and some of the literature that she said she had included was missing. He told me that he had opened all my letters and that I would not receive any that contained any biblical passages, hymns, or anything to do with Christianity.

I was enraged! *Who was he to take control of my private affairs,* I wondered. I realized that he had also opened letters that I had written and given him to mail. He was the middleman for my letters going and coming. Many, if not all, of them were probably never mailed. I was so hurt that my privacy had been invaded and that I was bereft of anything to call my own.

Mohamed was determined to dictate how I lived my life, and he told me that he was going to have the officials check all the mail that came addressed to me. There was no way that he would allow his children to be exposed to any Christian literature. I resolved to find some way to get my letters mailed in the future. I could no longer trust Mohamed to mail them. I needed to stay in touch with my family and praying friends, even if it was only for my sanity. It was imperative that the lines of communication were kept open, and with that determination and a fighting spirit within me I sought the Lord, demanding that He find a way for me lest the mission He had brought me here for would not get accomplished. The Lord admonishes us to bring our strong reasons to Him and to present our case to Him (Isaiah 41:21), and I did just that—reverently, of course.

Probably because of the stress I was undergoing, I began to experience a general illness over my entire body, and this led me to seek out treatment at the local clinic. It was there that I met several Christian nurses, most of whom were Catholic. I was so overjoyed to have come across other Christians, there was no time for prejudice. The differences between our denominations seemed unimportant. I was just so happy to find another believer in Jesus Christ who spoke English.

Katherine (one of the nurses) and I quickly became friends, and she invited me to her home. I would visit with her from time to time, and on one occasion my two daughters accompanied me to her home, and I introduced them. I met her husband and ten-month-old baby daughter. Sometimes we would visit the park together with my two little girls while Mohamed was at the mosque with the boys, praying.

Katherine and her husband worked hard as the breadwinners for their large family back in the south of India. Each month they would send money home. Katherine told me of the secret underground churches that would meet on Sundays for worship. I was interested but not willing to overextend myself into what could be presumption; besides, I wasn't quite sure how safe it all was.

About this time Katherine introduced me to Dr. Rassolpur, one of the doctors, who was also from South India. As our friendship developed, I told her about some of the hardships I had been facing and that communication with my family had been cut off. Amazingly, she understood and shared with me that there were many other women in my position. The laws, she said, are very tight and restrictive toward women. She suggested that I use her address to send and receive letters; she also offered to mail my letters. I thanked the Lord for hearing my prayers and making a way for me to reestablish contact with my family. So I began hiding the letters in the waistband of my clothing whenever I would go to the clinic.

At last I had contact with my family again. Now they knew what was going on with me in Saudi Arabia, and I was able to receive letters of encouragement from friends and family members. Just knowing that someone out there was praying for me brought such comfort. My mother even mailed a parcel for me that I brought home a little at a time without Mohamed knowing. It was filled with good things to eat that we had been missing.

As Katherine and I grew closer, she expressed an interest in learning some of the doctrines in my religious beliefs. Once again a spirit of gratitude to God filled my soul, and I could see another reason for our friendship. This gave me a sense of hope that I wasn't called here to simply suffer and that God had a plan for my life in Arabia.

We made arrangements to begin our studies, but we were only able to get through one lesson before the way was hedged up and made difficult. I returned to the clinic a few days later only to find that Katherine wanted no contact with me and made a conscious effort to avoid me. For a moment I wondered whether my medical test results had indicated that I had contracted some highly contagious disease. I asked, "What's wrong, Katherine?"

She pushed away and begged me, "Go, go! Leave me alone."

When I left the clinic, I did not go home right away but waited outside until Katherine's shift was over. I wanted to find out what I had done to deserve her reaction to me. Several hours later she came through the door, saw me, and quickly ran to the other side of the street, walking swiftly toward her house. I started to follow her, inquiring why she was acting this way. She said, "You stay on that side of the street. Do not walk with me. Please leave me alone."

I was determined to find out what was wrong and followed her all the way home. As she turned into her apartment building, I chased her up the stairs. She went into the building and slammed the door in my face. I banged on the door and continued banging until she finally opened it and peered through the crack. She whispered, "If I tell you, will you leave?"

"Yes, of course," I said. She went on to say that Mohamed had come to their home with the police, accusing her family of pushing Christianity in the country and on his family. He also accused them of running a prostitution ring. The authorities believed the story, simply because they were a Christian family. They locked her husband in jail and cautioned her that if she were ever seen with me again, she would be executed.

We had to terminate our friendship immediately for the sake of her family in India, and our lives. The next time I went to the clinic I took a little gift for her. It was a pamphlet containing the Ten Commandments and also a note that read, "The Holy Spirit will be your teacher, Katherine; after all, He is the best."

Katherine's husband was released from jail within the next few days.

Shortly after that, the news about Mohamed and his dealings with Katherine's family spread among the workers in the clinic. It finally reached the ears of Dr. Rassolpur, and she became afraid of Mohamed and the power he seemed to have. She decided that it was too risky for her to continue the favor of letting me use her mailing address. I understood the difficulties; these people were innocent, and they couldn't risk losing their positions as professionals, because they were not the only ones involved—they also had a duty to send money to their poor families back in India. This was so hard to take. I couldn't help but feel resentment toward Mohamed. Once again, communication with my family ceased.

I felt so alone and so isolated from the real world. I realized that my world was again reduced to the apartment that we had recently moved into. It was just the Lord and me. I could not share with anyone else the torment that I was going through. No one else could understand my innermost feelings; this was indeed a spiritual warfare between the arch-deceiver and Christ Jesus. I couldn't even pray. I just sat wondering if this was all real. I kept thinking, *I'll wake up any moment now and find myself still a little girl, an innocent little girl in my nice warm bed in my parents' home, awakening from a terrible nightmare.* But God gently nudged me back to reality. Even though I often felt too discouraged to pray, I know now that the Holy Spirit was able to translate the cry of my heart into a beautiful prayer.

I often read the book of Psalms, where I found much comfort in quiet meditations. Heaven was not so far away then, and my life became a little more tolerable. The Lord always sent His comforting Spirit to minister to my broken spirit. Jesus promises that He will not leave us comfortless. I begged the Lord to not leave my side, and He would remind me of His leading in our past together, of His presence, and of the fact that He had never left me before and never would. You see, we have nothing to fear for the future, except as we forget the way He has led in the past. I praised God for the miracle of getting my Bible through customs. How could I have survived this test without His Word to lighten this dark path and to give me the courage that I so needed to press on and hold fast to my faith to the end?

chapter 9

A Great Loss

The city of Damman is a very orthodox city; it is an old city with few modern sites. My surroundings were a constant reminder of the complete isolation that I was experiencing. I was cut off from my family and cut off from the friendships that I had tried to develop in my brief and infrequent contact with other persons outside my immediate family. Mohamed was not sensitive or sympathetic to my needs. He had become more aggressive and had lost all tenderness toward me. I felt like a servant, someone to care for the needs of Mohamed and the children.

However, I continued to study the Word of God with the children. This was my only means of escape from the awful depression that was seeking to control me. I found calm assurance in God's Word. I found peace and comfort there. I kept in constant communion with God; prayer became the essence of my life. Not only should we pray for ourselves, we should walk humbly in the light that we have received. The Lord turned things around for Job when he began to pray for his enemies. When he desired that those who had opposed him might be helped of God, Job received help from the Lord. We must keep before the Lord those who hurt us and continue to hurt us. We must pray without ceasing, pray, pray, for God does not rest. Pray in your heart and out loud. God hears the prayer of the sincere heart. My favorite Christian writer says in her book,

> Let all who are afflicted or unjustly used, cry to God. Turn away from those whose hearts are as steel, and make your requests known to your Maker. Never is one repulsed who comes to Him with a contrite heart. Not one sincere prayer is lost. Amid the anthems of the celestial choir, God hears the cries of the weakest human being. We pour out our heart's desire in our closets, we breathe a prayer as we walk by the way, and our words reach the throne of the Monarch of the universe. They may be inaudible to any human ear, but they cannot die away into silence, nor can they be lost through the activities of business that are going on. Nothing can drown the soul's desire. It rises above the din of the street, above the confusion of the multitude, to the heavenly courts. It is God to whom we are speaking, and our prayer is heard (*Christ's Object Lessons*, 174).

How comforting are these words. Our prayers will be answered—

> Ask, then; ask, and ye shall receive. Ask for humility, wisdom, courage, increase of faith. To every sincere prayer an answer will come. It may not come just as you desire, or at the time you look for it; but it will come in the way and at the time that will best meet your need. The prayers you offer in loneliness, in weariness, in trial, God answers, not always according to your expectations, but always for your good (*Gospel Workers*, 258).

I often wondered about the spiritual life of my children and how they were doing under all the pressure. They missed their family members and friends from school. They seemed to have adjusted pretty well to their new lifestyle. They occupied themselves well. They became very creative and made toys out of old newspapers; they played among themselves; there were laughter and the usual fights. As the evening would cool off, they would go outside to play with some of the neighborhood children. They would spot the lizards and chase them and examine the dead bodies of huge winged roaches.

One evening the children left to go play outside as usual; they returned after a while, very excited to share with me their findings. They had met a Hindu man from India who came up to them and asked if their parents needed a servant and said that he would be willing to work for us because he needed a job. They promised that they would ask.

During the course of their conversation, the man realized that the children were not Arabs, even though they looked like Arab children. Their English was too good, and it gave them away. The man proceeded to question the boys as to where they came from and what religion they were. He was surprised when the boys said they were Christians and asked him about his religion. The man said, " 'I am a Hindu,' " and he began to tell them what his religion was all about and the many gods they served, how they would carve and make their gods and then turn around and pray to them.

The children told him that they thought it strange to create a god and then pray to him, and they went on to say, "Shouldn't the god pray to you? After all, you did create him, therefore you are greater than him; in fact, you are his creator." The man looked puzzled, to say the least.

The children went on to tell him that their God whom they serve is the greatest because He created the whole universe and everything in it, including the materials used to make the Hindu gods. Then the man said that Hindus worship the cow and do not eat cows' flesh. The children looked at the man with an innocent, puzzled look on their faces and said, "We don't. We worship the Lamb—the Lamb of God—he takes all our sins away. Then they went on to explain the ceremonial laws and the transfer of sins to an innocent animal and how that animal would be sacrificed in order for the sins of that person to be forgiven. They went on to say that when Jesus came to earth, He took the title "the Lamb of God" because sin was all over the earth, and there were not enough lambs to keep sacrificing. So God sent His only Son to be that last Lamb, the ultimate Lamb that would die for everyone's sins, which He did when He died on the cross, and the curtain in the temple was torn from top to bottom—from the top because God did it, and He is up in heaven.

I was in utter amazement as I looked at these little boys and heard the story of redemption in the most simplistic language. They continued, "The man was so interested, Mom, he just stood there and listened. We told him that at that point when the curtain was torn, the ceremonial laws were done away with, and now by our acceptance of Jesus in our lives and believing that He is the last Lamb to have been sacrificed for our sins, we can still be forgiven.

" 'How do you do that?' " the man asked.

"Well," said the children, "we do that by praying to Jesus and telling Him what we did wrong. Believing that He is the symbol of a lamb, we place our sins on Him, and He takes them from us, and we receive His forgiveness." I looked at my children with a sense of wonder—they were so innocent and so happy. They had witnessed to someone, and I knew that God had a purpose for them too. My eyes filled with tears as I witnessed the Holy Spirit's presence in their individual lives. I realized I had nothing to fear concerning my children. God showed me they were His, and all my teachings were not in vain. God had written His word on their hearts, and they were thoroughly convinced of their belief in God the Creator.

"Well, we told the man that we had no need for a servant at that time, but we thanked him for his offer." I told the children how proud I was that they stood up for their faith.

The next day I was impressed to teach the children about Joseph and how as an innocent child he was taken from his secure home into a life of uncertainty. Joseph remembered his parents' teaching and trusted in the great God of heaven and earth. He missed his parents; he felt afraid at times, but he held fast to his faith and believed that God would rescue him. We were able to identify with the story, and the children and I pledged to remain faithful to God if we were ever separated.

One evening during our family worship, the children and I were discussing the remnant church of God and how to identify it. The children were particularly interested in this subject. We became so engrossed in the topic that the time slipped away from us and we forgot that Mohamed would be home any minute. We had a watchman at the window, and it was strange that Mohamed had not arrived at his usual time. Mohamed was smart, and he figured that I was still teaching the children, so that particular evening he parked the car farther down the street and walked the rest of the way, taking the back stairs. He must have been outside the door for half an hour or more when suddenly it flew open, and in walked a raging Mohamed. There was no time to put the books away. We were caught!

Fear was written over the faces of the children as they waited to see what would happen next. I calmly collected the books and, holding them close to my chest, walked past Mohamed toward the bedroom. I could feel his anger and hatred toward me. The presence of evil in the apartment was very real, and it caused us to fear. I tried not to show my fear so that the children would not be afraid.

As I put the books away, Mohamed met me at the door of the bedroom and said, "So you continue to teach them, huh? I don't want my children to know about this evil religion of yours!"

I kept silent because I believed that any response to that type of rage would have caused a terrible scene. He was following me around and literally breathing down my neck with clenched fists. Had I argued back or opened my mouth, I surely would have died that night. It was as though he was daring me to speak so he could have an excuse to beat me.

I quickly slipped by Mohamed as he continued shouting angry words while following me. I didn't think that he would harm the children, but I was uncertain of what he would do to me. I feared for my life and quickly moved into the bathroom and locked the door. As I stood there trembling, not knowing what would happen next, I could hear things being thrown around. I wondered, *What now, Lord?* I began to pray, "Lord this is an emergency! Please come to our rescue!"

All of a sudden, I heard the front door slam shut. Soon the children were knocking on the bathroom door. "Mom, Mom," they called, "you can come out now. Papa's gone." They went on to tell me that Mohamed had taken my Bible and all of my books, tapes, and other literature with him. I was so upset, so angry! I felt stripped of my only resources, power-less and debilitated. Truly, I thought, all was lost.

It was with a very heavy heart that I put the children to bed that night. I went into my room, fell on my knees, and had a serious talk with the Lord. I told him exactly how I felt. I was so wronged, so oppressed, so bewildered. I had no control over any part of my life. I thought I was losing my mind. I prayed for my sanity. I couldn't understand the intense suffering. *Why, God? Why?* I was like the children of Israel. God would do great things for me, and then something would happen, and I would end up complaining, my faith wavering. But then the calming, comfort-ing words of Scripture—passages that I had stored in my mind—began to unfold in my ears. "Thou wilt keep him in perfect peace, whose mind is stayed on thee: because he trusteth in thee" (Isaiah 26:3). And with the sweet communion of the Holy Spirit ministering to my distraught soul, I fell into a peaceful, tranquil sleep.

When I awoke the next morning, I prayed and asked the Lord to bring back to my memory all the lessons He had taught me so that I could con-tinue to share His Word with the children. Family worship that morning was truly wonderful. God brought back to our minds so many beautiful truths. We spoke about the Holy Spirit. We remembered Scriptures and quotations from the Spirit of Prophecy, and we were comforted and spiritu-ally motivated to face the challenges of the day. We continued to worship God, and we witnessed the Lord bringing back to our memory that which we had spent time studying and memorizing. Just as He had promised in His Word.

We were thankful that we had taken the time to store His words in our hearts, for if there was nothing in the vessel, nothing could be re-turned. God had said in His words, "My people are destroyed for lack of knowledge" (Hosea 4:6). We were happy that we had the knowledge of Him. The children were very excited about the fact that every time we gathered for family worship, the Holy Spirit would bring us a topic to discuss. Our worship periods were very inspiring and meaningful.

chapter 10

Silent Witnesses

After about a week, I started getting anxious again. I began to get very impatient with God. He had given me a work to do in Saudi Arabia, and I didn't have the tools to do the job, or so I thought. I began searching for my books—surely God would not really allow Mohamed to destroy those books. I looked everywhere I could think of in and around the apartment. I looked to no avail, in all the unlikely places such as in the trash. I walked through the streets praying and talking to the Lord and asking Him to lead me to my books and checking out the trash cans at the same time. I just could not believe they were gone. Alas, I returned to the apartment with a heavy heart and tear-filled eyes, pleading with the Lord for endurance.

Isn't it funny how, when we think that we've given our problems over to God, we soon find that we have picked them up again without even realizing it. Suddenly we feel the pressure building again, and distrust in God steadily builds as our burdens begin to get heavier and heavier. Then we get crushed under the weight and cry out for help from God once again. God is so very patient with us.

I had just finished preparing dinner when the children bounded into the apartment. Mohamed had brought them back from afternoon prayers and then returned to the office. I could tell they were excited and had some good news to tell me. What I heard next amazed me tremendously. Mohamed had taken my books to the office where he worked. The children said all of the men were reading them and discussing the gospel truths among themselves.

My joy couldn't be contained. I jumped up and praised God for what He had done. He had taken those books to those men, knowing full well that I, as a woman, could not go where those men were. Seeds of truth were being sown in their minds—truths that one day, by God's grace, will germinate. What a tremendous outcome this was! I reflected on how angry I had been at God that He allowed my books to be taken. And yet, out of evil came good. I began to praise and thank Him for using me in some small way to be His witness.

God is to be praised for His wisdom. He knows what to do and the right time in which to do His mighty acts. Oh, how we need to trust Him more. God does not afflict us, but He works in us and through us to accomplish His purposes even when our faith is weak. I felt as though I was constantly having new beginnings with God. I was always repenting and asking for forgiveness. I was getting tired of myself, but God assured me that He was never tired of me, for this is what a life of sanctification really is. If we fail to go to God after we have fallen, then we will be lost and the feeling of unworthiness will overcome us. This is the devil's tactic to make us feel that God is tired of our shortcomings and repetitive sins.

That evening, I could not wait to tell Mohamed that I knew where he had taken my books, but as soon as I had spoken, I knew I had done the wrong thing. I had spoken without consulting the Lord. I should have been more patient. I told myself that I should have waited on the Lord to complete what He had begun with those books. Mohamed became furious and called the children traitors. He ordered one of the girls to get a shoe so he could beat the three boys. She obeyed nervously. We watched as he held the boys up one by one by their legs and beat them unmercifully. He beat the oldest more than he beat the twins. They screamed and cried. When I could no longer stand by and watch, I jumped in the middle of the fray and tried to stop Mohamed. I yelled, "It's not their fault! Stop beating them! You should beat me instead. Leave them alone!"

It was a scene of confusion. There was screaming and crying. It was awful! Somehow, I managed to pull Mohamed off the boys. He turned and gave me a blow to the face, cutting my lip against my teeth. My sons yelled out, "Mommy, don't say anything more! Please, Mommy, be quiet!" They apparently felt that my being quiet would stop the rage of their father. The desperation in their faces tugged at my heart, and I calmed myself down for their sakes. I walked out of the room. Truly, this was a night I would never forget.

A couple of days later, my books started to reappear, one by one. First, I found my Bible, and then the other books and literature followed, along with my personal cassette player. The men at the office had torn up a few of the small books. The children later told me that their father had rescued the returned books from being destroyed by the men. How happy I was to see those books again! It was like being reunited with long-lost friends.

Sadness seemed to be my constant companion. There was always a trial to replace the previous one conquered. I was physically and mentally drained, and the days that followed were especially difficult. I was growing tired of being indoors, so I decided that I would take the children to a nearby park where I could read while they played. It was extremely hot, but I felt the need to get outside for a while. Time seemed to go by ever so slowly; the days just lingered on. It's very rare for a woman to be seen outdoors alone with children in Saudi Arabia. In fact, a woman places herself in grave danger of rape or kidnap by going out.

There is crime in Saudi Arabia, but it's generally not reported by the media. The Saudis have very strict laws established by the religion of Islam. As part of Saudi tradition, on Fridays after the noon prayers, the entire family would eat and then go to the seaside to play, swim, and enjoy each other's company, or they would go to the parks. However, Fridays were also set aside for open-air executions, and on some Fridays this was what took place.

One particular Friday, the children and I saw a crowd of people in the city center. We inquired what was going on and were told that an execution had just taken place. Three robbers who had raped and killed their victims were publicly hanged in the streets as families with young children looked on. The families were encouraged to bring their children to witness executions as a deterrent to criminal behavior.

I had made up my mind that the children and I would be better off leaving Saudi Arabia, so I began to take things into my own hands and try to help God along. On one of our walks, I decided to try to get in touch with the U.S. and/or British Embassy to see if someone could possibly help the children and me get out of the country. I was so happy when I finally figured out how to use the telephone. After spending what seemed like a lot of money, I finally made a connection with the U.S. Embassy. I related my experiences, but to my distress, the embassy official apologetically told me that he was unable to help me and that there were many women in similar conditions here in Saudi. I was so brokenhearted. It was little comfort to learn that others were experiencing a similar fate.

I was wrapped up in my disappointment when, suddenly, I heard the children shouting "Papa, Papa." Sure enough, Mohamed had just driven up. He had obviously been looking for us. I did not expect him home this early. I had planned to be back home by the time he got back. He stormed angrily out of the car and started to grab the children and place them forcibly in the car. Then he drove off, leaving me standing there alone and in shock.

I was afraid to go home; yet, I had to because the children needed me. "Oh, God," I prayed, "Where are You?" Whatever the outcome, I knew that God had promised never to leave me nor forsake me, and He would not permit me to endure more than I could bear. With the confidence that God was at my side, I made my way home. Mohamed met me at the door and took the keys to the apartment from me. From then on, I was a prisoner in the apartment. He locked the apartment every time he left home. He took the children to work with him every day; my time with the children was now very limited.

I remained in constant communion with God, pleading for my children and the influences they were being exposed to. Every time I needed a comforting word, God would speak through His Word. He said, "My sheep hear my voice," and I learned to recognize His voice as I never had before. Hallelujah!

chapter 11

Mother's Love Tested

Mohamed had made no secret of his intentions to convert our sons to the Islamic religion. He spoke often of his plans for our three boys.

The Lord kept me ahead of things by giving me dreams. In one dream, I was in the car with my children. Suddenly, I saw them being taken away, and, for some unknown reason, I was unable to turn and help them. I was left with my two daughters only. I clung to their hands, and now we were walking on a very narrow path. All around me was darkness and gloom. I looked up and saw a heart descending from heaven. As it came closer, I recognized that it consisted of angels, and at the apex there were two pillars containing the commandments. The heart signified love. "If you love me, keep my commandments," were the instructions. I continued on the narrow path, being careful not to let my feet slip or my daughters lose their grip and sink down into the valley below. I woke up very troubled.

On November 26, 1989, Mohamed awoke and said that he was taking the children with him for a trip to the beach. Although this was unusual, I did not object. As they were about to leave, he sent them back for their light jackets. I could not understand why they needed jackets, because it

57

was very hot outside. I whispered to Adam that I felt uneasy as if something was about to happen, but Adam looked at me and said, "Don't worry, Mom, everything will be all right." They left, and I watched until the car disappeared from view. Deep down inside I suspected that something was wrong.

About nine o'clock that evening, there was a knock on the door. I answered the door to find Sammy and Mona standing there, both wearing very sad expressions on their faces. I invited them in. Taking a seat, they broke the news to me that the boys had left for Medina with their father to begin classes at an Islamic boarding school. I wept bitterly as I inquired about my daughters. They assured me that the girls were all right and were at their house. As I left with them to be reunited with the girls, Sammy handed me an envelope containing a note from Mohamed. It said, "Sorry I had to do it this way, but if I hadn't, you would have created such a scene. I'll be back in ten days. Here is three hundred riyals to buy food."

I couldn't believe what was happening to me. Was I dreaming? I didn't even get to say goodbye to my sons. How could Mohamed do this to me? Returning home, I went into the boys' bedroom and gazed at the mattresses and their clothes. Everything was so quiet, so empty. All their clothes were there. They had not even taken their toothbrushes. But they were gone—gone far away.

As the days went by, I prayed earnestly to the Lord for the safety of my sons. I prayed that Mohamed would rethink what he had done and bring the boys safely home again. For ten days I waited. The moments just seemed to crawl by. When the tenth day finally came, I waited anxiously for the doorbell to ring, expecting to see Mohamed with my three sons at his side. But that day came and went as the first nine had come and gone with no word from Mohamed.

The next day I arose early, dressed the girls, and walked to Mohamed's place of employment. I covered my face when the men walked by. I knew it must have been a strange sight to them to see me just standing in the hallway with my two daughters. The men seemed disgusted to see some woman standing there in the lobby—this was not accepted—but I didn't care at this point. I was desperate to know where my sons were. At last I saw one of Mohamed's friends and asked whether he had heard from Mohamed. "Where are my boys? When is he coming home? He was supposed to come yesterday." He told me that they had heard nothing from Mohamed. I left and went back home disappointed.

Two weeks went by, four weeks, then six weeks—still no word from my sons, no sign of Mohamed. I continued to go to his office three or four times per week, hoping to hear something, anything. By now I didn't care what the men thought of me. I just wanted to know where my sons were. The money my husband had left lasted only two weeks. The food at our house had run out, and now my daughters and I were facing hunger, starvation, and certain death unless there was some kind of intervention. It was now winter, and the apartment was very cold.

I was getting more and more desperate. I couldn't speak the language, so I prayed and asked God for wisdom to know what to do to obtain food for my daughters. I had to do something. After all, the girls were dependent upon me. I remembered Psalm 37:25, "I have been young, and now am old; yet have I not seen the righteous forsaken, nor his seed begging bread." This encouraged me, and I was assured that God would not let us go hungry.

I took the empty canisters that had contained rice and oil and other grocery items and began knocking on the doors of the people in the neighborhood. When I showed them the empty canisters, they knew exactly what I needed and filled them up. One neighbor was so generous that she cooked us a hot meal on several occasions and sent us hot food on a tray, along with fruits and vegetables. This neighbor also helped me to get a few letters out to my family.

Just as the Lord had sent the ravens to feed Elijah, He sent various persons to feed us. The Lord multiplied everything we had, and my daughters started to gain weight.

After two months of isolation, anxiety, and sleepless nights, I was mentally ready to kill Mohamed for what he had done. I even pictured myself running a knife through his heart and feeling satisfied to see him die. The Lord had to do something for me.

In waiting, I realized that there were many lessons that I needed to learn. I learned during that period of time that I needed love in my heart in order to be an overcomer, not hatred or anger. I needed the love of God, *agape* love, to help me deal with the hostility that I was feeling toward Mohamed. I began to see how desperately wicked I really was. I was not pleased with the person I saw in me. All along I thought that I was a good Christian woman, doing good for all. But now I came face to face with my true self.

I was a murderer, ready to kill one of God's created beings. I was so ashamed of myself when God pointed these things out to me and showed me that His concern was for my soul's salvation. I needed cleansing. God had to clean me up and remove all the dross of sin.

There were so many sinful character traits in my life that were previously masked by my self-righteousness. The circumstances had brought these sins to the surface, and I was surprised to know how far I had fallen. The Scriptures say that when we think we stand, we fall. This was a most humbling experience, and I saw that I was no better than Mohamed. During the waiting period, God tested my patience and showed me that love would be the only weapon that could give me the victory. It was a fierce battle with self, but I chose to love. I began to spend many hours on my knees, talking with the Lord, asking Him for strength to face my trials and for direction on how to receive and treat Mohamed whenever he returned.

The girls and I decided to visit Zainup, and we made a habit of going to see her at least once or twice a week. The girls would play with their children and have a good time. Zainup and I would cook together and prepare meals and then eat together. We talked about America and the lifestyle we both missed. I learned a lot about her family and how she had met and married her Syrian husband. We would often take walks to the grocery store. Zainup was very sympathetic toward me and understood my difficulty. As we got better acquainted, she began to tell me about the physical abuse she was suffering from her husband. She could never do anything right, and he constantly threatened to take a second wife. We became friends, and she allowed me to tell her of my experiences with the Lord and share with her the gospel story. Most importantly, I shared that Jesus loved her and was watching over her.

That Christmas was a very lonely time for the girls and me. It was difficult to get into the spirit of Christmas. The warm feelings that Christmas brings were lacking as we sat in one room of the apartment that we had made our home. We cuddled together under the blankets and thought of my family back home and the joys that Christmases past had brought.

A week later we ushered in the new year and that, too, was nothing to get excited about. We were feeling distressed, not knowing where or how the boys were. The girls really missed their brothers. They were trying so hard to make the best of a bad situation, even at such a young age. They began to play with three imaginary friends whose names were Shannon, Hackis, and Lena. They played intensely, dressing up and finding anything and everything to laugh at. At times they would sit quietly and suck their thumbs. I could see that they were mourning the absence of their brothers and father. At other times I would observe them sighing; then they would put their heads in my lap and ask me to tickle them. They needed to laugh. As the Bible says, "A merry heart doeth good like a medicine."

So, even though my own heart was aching, I would reach for them and run my fingers over their ribs. This took great effort on my part, and I often would look away in sadness and tears. I didn't want the girls to see me crying. I didn't want to add to their misery. At night when we slept together, the girls would put me between them and ask me to tell them story after story and read to them. It was difficult for me because I was also grieving. It took a lot of effort. But I forced myself to do it for their sake.

chapter 12

Trying Times

On January 11, 1990, Mohamed returned. I greeted him with open arms and a kiss on his cheek. My heart was filled with divine love—not my love, but God's love for him. As he walked in, I peered outside to see if the boys were hiding behind the door to surprise me. But the hallway was empty, and my heart sank to its lowest depths.

The girls were all over Mohamed as he unpacked. Daddy was home, and they were very happy to see him. I started to prepare him something to eat and inquired about the boys. He insisted that they were fine; they had settled in and were happy, he assured me. I didn't believe him for one moment. How could they be happy away from the only home and family they knew?

That night Mohamed slept in the boys' bedroom. It was cold in there. We had two portable heaters that Sammy had given us to use, but because just the girls and I were in the apartment, we only kept one room warm. As I prepared to go to bed with the girls, my heart was moved with compassion toward Mohamed sleeping in a cold room. So I took one of the heaters and placed it in the room next to him so that he could be warm and comfortable. I went back and fell asleep with the girls.

The next day, he informed me that he was leaving in four days for the capital city of Riyadh, where he said he had a job offer. So four days later, he left us again with a promise to visit us weekly or bi-weekly. It was obvious that he didn't want us with him. He didn't offer to take us. As I saw him leave, my heart was saddened at the thought of the loneliness I would again encounter. I had no choice but to accept his decision.

At the end of every week, which in Saudi Arabia falls on Wednesday, I grew hopeful that Mohamed would be home. Over and over again through the day, I went to the window expecting to see his car. Riyadh was about a three-hour journey away. Invariably, however, as the mornings gave way to afternoons and the afternoons changed to evening and then to night, my anxiety would turn to despair.

I longed for the company of another adult. I enjoyed the company of my girls, but I needed someone to talk to on an adult level. I was so tired of simply playing with the girls; I needed adult conversation, even if it was with someone who was as cruel to me as Mohamed was. As the twilight turned to darkness on the weekends, so did my soul. I lived for the sound of Mohamed's key in the lock. He had a habit of not letting me know when he was coming home. Therefore, every weekend was filled with anxiety as I anticipated his coming. Oftentimes we were let down when he never showed.

This went on for several weeks with no sight of Mohamed. The feeling of isolation started to consume me. I began having nightmares. I thought often of my sons and imagined them crying for me. Sometimes I would awaken in the middle of the night sweating profusely and crying to the Lord to watch over my boys. The mental anguish was almost maddening, and I constantly prayed for the Lord to preserve my sanity. God had promised to keep me in perfect peace, and I depended on Him to do just that.

The Lord showed me in a dream one night that I needed to pray more. To do this, I asked Him to awaken me in the early morning so that I could meet with Him and He and I could commune together. We didn't have an alarm clock, so I asked the Lord to awaken me each morning for prayer. God is so good! It was amazing the number of unusual ways He used to help me keep my appointment with Him. For instance, one morning I awoke with a headache; no sooner had I started to pray than the headache was gone. Some mornings I awoke with a toothache, only to have it disappear as I began talking to God. One morning my daughter came into the room and touched me then walked back to her room and went right back to sleep. Another time, I heard my mother's voice calling me. I jumped out of bed in response. It was time for prayer. I recognized the special attention of God in these occurrences. Each morning a special agent of God, through the Holy Spirit, awakened me until the waking pattern was established.

It became very real to me that I was the object of a fierce warfare between the forces of light and the forces of darkness, Christ versus Satan. As I read and studied the Word of God, my relationship with Him grew stronger, and I prayed for an experience that would bring me even closer to Him.

There were times when the warfare turned into a physical struggle for my life. Satan wanted me dead. During the night, as the girls slept, I awoke to a presence in the room. I sensed that my room was filled with demons, and I experienced indescribable fear. My bed rippled and shook as it slowly lifted off the floor. At other times I had the feeling that my entire life was being crushed out, and as I struggled to breathe, my chest walls felt as though they were caving in. Then I would cry out to the Lord in my mind, *Save me, save me! Jesus save me!*

The fear was so intense. I often experienced what felt like an electrifying jolt go through my body as if the hand of Satan were trying to claim me. I would beg the Lord, "Don't let him have the victory! Don't let him take my life." After a while, relief would come; I would hear the still, small voice of my Savior bidding me to stay calm and be assured that my life was in His hands. He spoke clearly; each time His voice was like medicine to my frail body, reviving me and giving me back my breath so that I could live.

It was abundantly clear to me that indeed "we wrestle not against flesh and blood, but against principalities, against powers, against the rulers of the darkness of this world, against spiritual wickedness in high places" (Ephesians 6:12).

65

Whenever there is a witness for God, Satan will seek to negate the witness and bring discouragement. He is an angry foe. Revelation 12:17 says, "And the dragon was wroth with the woman, and went to make war with the remnant of her seed, which keep the commandments of God, and have the testimony of Jesus Christ."

I can testify that Satan is not a myth or a fairy tale; He is real, just as God is real.

My experience was not always one of triumph. There were times when I felt I would rather die than go on living like this. Many days held nothing but pain and suffering. I began to prefer death to life. I spent long periods of time in dismay, peering through the window. Suicide seemed to be an acceptable alternative to the living death I was experiencing. On more than one occasion, I felt the impulse to throw the girls out the window and then jump behind them, bringing an end to the miserable life I was living. But each time, God sent the Holy Spirit and angels that excelled in strength to comfort me and save me from myself.

Emotionally, physically, and mentally, I had reached my lowest depths. I weighed only about 90 pounds, and my hair was falling out by the handfuls. I was weak from crying, agonizing, fasting, and praying at all hours of the day and night. In addition, I was grieving for my sons whom I had not heard from since they were taken from me. I was concerned about their well-being. I often got up in the middle of the night, impressed by God to pray for them. I would sense that something was wrong and would plead earnestly that God in His mercy would attend to all their needs.

This was a very trying time for me. I could hardly bear the thought of my sons suffering the way I was suffering. I begged God to let them die where they were and not to let them suffer. I pleaded, "Lord, take them. I would rather know that they were buried and sleeping in the ground away from this warfare. Why, God? Why are we suffering so?"

I reflected on my life and the way I had ignored God in the past. How I had left His side and made my own choices, disobeying His directions for my life. At first I was angry with God. I began to wonder whether He was punishing me for my past failures. The thought came to me that "the wages of sin is death; but the gift of God is eternal life" (Romans 6:23). I could have died out there in the world, and I deserved to. But God in His tender mercy did not give me what I deserved; instead, He offered me eternal life. He placed a hedge of protection around me when I was not aware of His presence.

It suddenly occurred to me how blessed I was to have a praying mother. Thank God for praying mothers! My mother is a special lady, a woman of faith, who never stopped interceding for me. Because of her prayers, I believe I was protected from the evils of the world that can cause death. This realization brought me to my senses. So I turned and gave God praise for sparing a wretch like me.

I realized for the first time that my children were not my own, and I asked God for forgiveness for praying for their death. I was convicted by the Holy Spirit that I was wrong, that selfishness was at the root of a prayer like that, and that I was not trusting in God as I should. I wanted to make things easier for me to bear. However, I knew that God understood my heart, and I refused to live under guilt. God had forgiven me.

chapter 13

Tempted and Tried

On one of the few weekends that Mohamed came to see us, he brought with him an imam to try to convert me to Islam. Imams are the very holy men in Islam and the leaders in the mosque. They have memorized all the Quran and all the prayers. They wear very long beards in order to make themselves distinguished among the people. To my surprise, this man brought three different versions of the Bible with him. I asked him how he managed to get so many Bibles in a country where Christianity was prohibited. He laughed and said, "I am a Muslim, an imam. I can use the Bible to prove Christianity wrong." Then he went on to show me what seemed to him to be contradictions in the Scriptures.

As he was speaking, I was praying to God for wisdom regarding how to respond. Obviously satisfied with his presentation, he sat back proudly and waited for me to challenge him. I looked in his eyes and heard myself sharing with him all that Jesus Christ had done for me and expressing confidence in what He was doing for me even now. I was filled with wisdom from God, I even taught myself a few things. I believe that the Holy Spirit was in complete control of the situation and was speaking through me in ways that astonished even me.

I could sense as I spoke that the imam was becoming more and more irritable. His impatience was growing and his kind demeanor shrinking rapidly. Shifting gears from an intellectual challenge to an emotional one, he retorted by asking, "Do you want your children back?"

"Yes, of course I do," was my quick response. "Why did you men decide to take them from me anyway? If you believe that your religion is the truth, why do you view me as a threat to you? After all, I'm just a weak, frail woman; I'm no challenge to you men." I pleaded with him to allow my sons to return. He promised to allow them to only if I took the "Shahadah." This is a profession of faith—"There is no god but Allah, and Mohammed is his prophet." These words initiate one into the religion of Islam.

I was sorely tempted to comply with his request. Thoughts raced through my mind as I considered the prospects of becoming a Muslim. I would get my sons back. Instantly, that was all that seemed to matter. I started to reason with God and to rationalize. After all, I thought, I could play the part of a Muslim woman. I knew exactly what to do and how to behave like one. The seeds of compromise were seeking a lodging place in my mind. I desperately wanted my sons back. I reasoned that I could behave like a Muslim, but God would know that my heart always belonged to Him. I felt that this was the only way I could have peace in my home and in my marriage again. My husband would love me again. My children would be returned to me. We would be a family again.

Several other imams came and visited with me, trying desperately to convince me to become a Muslim; they left me with audiotapes and books to study Islam. I listened and read with a very open mind, wanting to know truth, but nothing stayed in my heart like the word of God. The Bible was firmly rooted in my mind, and I couldn't have gotten rid of it even if I had tried.

These men would always use my sons to entice me to become Muslim. They would say, "If you only pray to Allah, you will have your sons back. . . . Don't you love them? . . . Then become a Muslim."

Eventually, I had to stop this torture. The matter was settled in my mind. I had prayerfully considered my options. I visualized my Savior being tempted after His baptism when He went into the wilderness to fast and pray to prepare for His earthly mission. It was when He was at His weakest point from fasting that Satan tempted Him. Yet He did not yield to the temptation. I was able to say as Christ had said at the height of His fierce battle with the enemy, "Get thee behind me, Satan."

I told Mohamed and the imams that they could keep my sons, because their words were no guarantee that I would ever see my children again, even if I changed my faith and accepted Islam. However, my faith in Jesus and trust in His promises and reliance on His Word gave me the assurance that if I never have the privilege of seeing my children on this earth again, I would still see them in the kingdom of heaven.

The men thought I had gone crazy; they told me that I did not love my children, but I responded that it was because I loved them that I could make this sacrifice.

Mohamed was totally embarrassed and threatened to have me committed to an asylum, but having taken my stand, I felt stronger physically, spiritually, and emotionally than I had felt in months. The imams were angry, disappointed, and surprised at my obstinacy, but I had resigned myself to my fate, and they left without saying another word.

I was unaware of it at the time, but it had taken all the strength I could muster to stand up to those imams. When they left, I was overwhelmed at the way the Spirit of God had used me. As the days went by, I missed my sons; I prayed for them and remembered all the good times we had had together. I asked the Holy Spirit to remind them of that special worship we had about Joseph so that they would continue in strength and trust that God would set them free one day.

One night I fell on my bed and began to sob uncontrollably. The mental and physical agony was like a dark cloud all around me, and I couldn't seem to see my way out. I cried out to God, asking Him, "Carry me, carry me, oh Lord." I crawled around on my hands and knees because I was too weak to stand. Once again I asked God why I had to suffer so much, and didn't He think that I had had more than my fair share; "God, why are You doing this to me?" I was angry at God, and I wanted Him to know it. "You can't comfort me," I shouted. "My children are gone. I thought You said 'Suffer the little children to come unto me.' Where are mine that I gave to You? Nothing can comfort me. This agony is too deep even for You, God, to comfort me. Why don't You just let me die?"

As I lay there, my insides aching almost unbearably, my wailing eventually turned to sobs, and I began to see visions of Calvary. I saw Christ on the cross and realized that His suffering was far greater than mine. He suffered for the sins of the whole world. He carried not only my sins to the cross but the sins of every past, present, or future inhabitant of the earth. His glory flashed before me as I lifted my head and reached for my Bible. I pulled it close to me. My eyes were brimming with tears as I opened it and searched to hear His sweet, tender voice speaking to me. The pages fell open at Jeremiah 31; it so happened that this was the very book of the Bible I had been reading for my personal devotions.

I read through the chapter, but nothing was making sense to me. I pleaded with God to speak to me. I desperately needed to hear His voice. My eyes began to focus on verses 15 through 17, and I recognized that God had again come through with just the words I needed to hear. He said, "Thus saith the LORD; a voice was heard in Ramah, lamentation, and bitter weeping; Rahel weeping for her children refused to be comforted for her children, because they were not. Thus saith the LORD; refrain thy voice from weeping, and thine eyes from tears: for thy work shall be rewarded, saith the LORD; and they shall come again from the land of the enemy. And there is hope in thine end, saith the LORD, that thy children shall come again to their own border."

Immediately, my eyes were opened. I felt a surge of new life go through my weak, frail body. I was living again; hope had sprung to life. I felt that the morning of my victory had just dawned, and I thanked and praised God and asked His forgiveness for ever doubting Him. I now knew that God had never left me; He had always been there carrying me through those times when I felt most alone and distressed. He had heard my cry and responded.

I was encouraged to press on. I trusted that my children were going to be returned to me. I did not know when this would all take place. But for now, I treasured the joy and assurance of knowing that all things were in God's hands.

God gave me the fortitude to continue to witness for Him in my home. I had to be strong for the girls, and it was important that I be a faithful witness to Mohamed.

By this time, however, I had had enough of Saudi Arabia. Day after day I stood at the window and prayed earnestly for God to send an army to rescue me and my children. This seemed to me to be the only way out, since I had no money and no other tangible means of escaping with my children. I had no doubt that my God had the power to do whatever He wanted to do for His children. As Christ's followers, we are the apple of His eye. As His children, we are special in His sight, and He is like a consuming fire unto the wicked, especially those who harm one of His own. In many ways, I felt sorry for Mohamed because he had no idea how great and powerful God was. I continued to worship the Lord while waiting for His deliverance.

Mohamed did not give up in his desire to convert me to Islam. He continued to send Islamic imams to speak to me. But each meeting gave me the opportunity for a wonderful witness as I shared with them what Jesus meant to me. These men came prepared, having studied the Bible in an effort to refute anything I had to say. Sometimes, they seemed more knowledgeable about the Bible than I was, but God gave me wisdom, and I became a vessel through which the Lord spoke. Whatever they asked, I was able to answer with intelligence and fluent speech. I had but to open my mouth, and the Lord filled it with the right words.

The imams often were very impatient, angry, and hostile toward me. After all, I was just a woman. In desperation and in an effort to save face, they challenged my love for my husband and children when I refused to embrace Islam.

chapter 14

News From Abroad

One weekend Mohamed returned from Riyadh for a visit with us. I wished he would stay, even though he hated being around me. I just longed for adult companionship and for someone to talk to who shared my language. Moving to Riyadh with him was out of the question. He said that he was not ready for us to move up there and that we might never be able to move with him because I was not a Muslim.

That weekend he took the girls to the mosque to pray while I remained at home. As I looked around the house, I noticed his briefcase sitting on the floor in the living room. A strange feeling of curiosity came over me as I walked toward the briefcase. I felt strongly impressed to open it. I hesitated at first but then yielded to impulse and began to look through its contents. I was not prepared for what I found. There were letters that I had written and given to Mohamed that had not been mailed. There were letters from my family that were never delivered to me. "God, how could this man be so cruel? I don't want to be in this marriage, but I have no way out." I pleaded with God, "If there is anything hidden, show me that I may have a way out of this marriage."

Beyond the Veil of Darkness

As I continued searching, I found an envelope postmarked in India. *How strange*, I thought to myself. *Who is he in contact with in India?* There was a letter written in English in the envelope with a cover letter written in Urdu, an Indian dialect. The handwriting of the letter written in English looked strangely familiar. On further examination, I noticed that there were three different handwritings in the letter and that the letter was written by my sons. They had taken one page, and each of them had written about five lines each. They were asking for their toys, and they wanted their "papa" and me to make up so that they could return home. They begged us not to forget them. My heart broke as I read their words.

By now my tears were flowing freely. I could hardly see, but I quickly scribbled the address down. Questions flooded my mind. Why were they in India? Mohamed had said that he had taken them to Medina. I had been lied to, and I didn't like it one bit. I didn't know what difference it would have made to know the truth all along, but I resented the fact that the little Mohamed had told me was a lie.

I continued to look through the briefcase and found another envelope. Inside was a card with the words "Wishing you were here" on the front. My heart started beating very fast. "Wishing you were here," I said to myself as I read the words. The sentiments expressed suggested that it was written by a woman who had spent some time with Mohamed in India. They obviously had had an affair. I quickly scratched that address down too, and with both addresses in hand, I closed the suitcase and stood up.

My knees were weak, my body sapped of every ounce of energy. I felt as if the blood had been drained from my body. I began pacing back and forth, wondering what to do next. What were my options? One idea that came to my mind was to befriend Mohamed and ask him to allow me to return home to renew my alien registration card, which was about to expire. This plan, I thought, would allow me to get help for my sons in India and plan for their escape. *But what would happen to the girls?* I wondered. Mohamed would never let me leave the country. If I could find a way to rescue the boys, I would probably lose the girls. Many thoughts raced through my mind. My heart was torn, my mind confused as I frantically paced up and down, asking God for direction.

My thoughts were interrupted by the sound of the key in the lock. I ran to the bedroom and hid the two addresses. I didn't know what to say. Then I decided to tell him the truth. He was very angry with me for going through his briefcase, but, sensing my pain and distress, he kept himself under control. He explained to me that the woman was a friend he had met in India and tried to assure me that the boys were truly all right. It seemed as if his heart was softening, and he began to talk about plans to move the girls and me to Riyadh where he had been working and living for the past couple months. Several weeks later we moved to Riyadh.

Riyadh was a welcome change. There were more diverse cultural influences there, and I felt more in touch with the world around me. Mohamed's cousins, who had returned from England some ten years previously, lived there. The husband was a doctor and his wife a homemaker. They were very pleasant. Even though they also were Muslims, they were not very strict adherents to the customs. They entertained friends from all over the world a great deal of the time.

It was at one of their dinner parties that I met Anna, a young British woman. She was married to a West Indian from Barbados, and they had two children. Anna's family was not practicing in any Christian religion, and they were not involved with Islam, but they remained open. She and I quickly became close friends, and I shared with her all that had taken place in my life since moving to Saudi Arabia. She admired my faith in God; we spent time together taking the children swimming in the ladies' pool and preparing meals together.

Shortly afterward, Mohamed had a telephone installed in the apartment, but long distance calls were restricted, and I was only able to call around Riyadh. I shared with Anna over the phone how I longed to hear from my family and to speak to my mother. She said she would call my family in England and let them know of my situation. She gave them my telephone number and advised them to call me at certain hours of the day when Mohamed was not at home. It was wonderful to get news from home and to communicate once again with my family. It was comforting to have them join me in prayer and fasting for the boys' safe return and for our safe release. Life in Arabia was a lot better in Riyadh because it was more international, and I felt more at home being able to communicate with adults who spoke my language and get some of the foods from back home. The Muslims here were not as strict and orthodox as those in Damman.

My heart still ached for my sons. Anna and I shared so much about the Lord, and her faith grew from day to day as we talked about God and the great things He had done for me. Anna wanted to help me escape. She couldn't stand to see me suffering anymore, so she called the embassies to inquire if there was anything they could do to help me leave the country with my daughters and find my sons in India. But the news from them was not hopeful; there was little they could do. Ultimately, the Saudis had the final word.

Anna continued calling friends in the United States to see what could be done for me. Someone gave her the number of a Christian group in Cyprus. The mission workers there were willing to send someone to help me escape through the desert and into Cyprus. Apparently they had helped people in the past. At first it sounded very exciting, and they wanted me to give them an idea of where we were located. I prayed about it, and I felt impressed that I was moving ahead of God. I didn't think that this was the escape that God in His providence had planned for me. I didn't want to leave Saudi Arabia feeling like a criminal escaping for my life.

I knew that God had sent me to Saudi Arabia on a mission to be a witness, and I felt honored to have a part to play in this great work. I should not have to escape as if I had done something wrong; there was no way that I was going to give Satan the glory by running in the night, scared and tormented, wondering if we would make it. No, I served a great God, One who would give me back my dignity and show Mohamed who is Lord and King. I felt sure that God would set me free when it was His time and when my work was done, and after my sons' return. I had not forgotten that night when God spoke to me in the words of Jeremiah. So

I continued to pray for grace, because He had said that His grace was sufficient.

I thanked Anna for her diligence and shared with her that it was not the will of God that we should leave by way of escape and that when God had finished using me here, He would do some great miracle to set us free. But I needed to wait for my sons to return and for us to all leave together side by side, with me looking across at all five children, watching them buckling up in their seats in the aircraft ready for takeoff. Anna understood, a mother herself, and admired my faith and trust in God.

chapter 15

Together Again

It had been six months since I had last seen my sons, and it was almost time for schools in India to begin the summer break. That reality brought an added sense of anticipation as I wondered where my boys would go when the boarding school closed for the summer. I hoped and prayed that Mohamed would let them come home, but he refused, saying that they would be spending the summer in the village of Vilpur with his family members.

God gave me the strength to bear this disappointment. I accepted my lot and pressed on, praying always for the love of God to reign in my heart and that I would continue to be a cheerful witness in my home.

One night, I dreamed I saw a young Indian woman. Her face was somewhat blurred in the dream, and she was crying for Mohamed. In the dream I also saw a passport picture of the same woman. I woke up feeling very despondent and troubled. Mohamed had told me that he had had no more contact with the woman he had met in India; but this dream really troubled me. In the past, the Lord had always talked to me in dreams, showing me many things; so I asked the Lord to make things clear to me.

Some time later, I found a telephone receipt with a phone number on it. When I compared the number with the one I had taken from

Mohamed's briefcase, it was the same. This confirmed to me that Mohamed was still communicating with this lady and that the friendship was still going on, even though I had written to her telling her that Mohamed was a married man.

Later that day Mohamed called the house, and I inquired of him whether or not he was still in contact with the Indian lady he had had the affair with. He denied it, but when I told him that I had the date and the telephone number to verify that he had called her, he was at a loss for words and began to confess, telling me that he was making plans for her to come to Saudi Arabia. I figured that was the reason I had seen the passport picture in my dream. She had been pressuring him to get back with her because she missed him so much. But was that any excuse to entertain the thought of making my life more miserable than it was? I asked him why he would even consider bringing her to Saudi Arabia, but He just laughed it off.

I was left to ponder the possibility that she might well become a second wife. In fact, he told me that he was thinking about getting married again to establish and preserve the Muslim influence in the home for the benefit of the children. He felt that it was the mother's duty to educate the children about Islam and that I was neglecting my duty because I was Christian. I was sad and afraid of what this would mean and prayed to God for courage and strength to deal with whatever might come my way.

Later I would learn what had happened to my sons while they were in India. They spent several weeks traveling around, looking for a suitable boarding school. They stopped at an Islamic school, but there were no children their age. The twins were eight and the older boy nine. The boys at that school were fifteen and above, so Mohamed's cousin who attended that school was assigned to be their caretaker. The boys were not happy; they missed home and felt very out of place. From that school they traveled to the village of Vilpur, where they stayed with cousins for a while. They helped out with the chores, fed the cattle, and played with the wild monkeys—which was not always a safe thing to do. They saw many unusual sights and adapted as much as possible to village life in India.

Together Again

One time my oldest boy almost got run over by a cart pulled by bulls. Another time he fell into a soft mud patch and barely made it out by gripping onto some grass that kept breaking off in his hands as he struggled to get out while his brothers ran for help. Then one of the twins became gravely ill with malaria and almost died. He was rushed to the hospital with tremors and a very high fever. It took some days for him to get back on his feet.

After a few weeks in the village it was time again for the boys to move on to another boarding school. By now the boys were tired of moving around and traveling on those slow, over-crowded trains. It was a tight, uncomfortable space for any child to be in over days at a time. At the news of having to leave, one of the boys ran screaming into the jungle. He had had enough, but the villagers chased after him and beat him for running away.

At the new boarding school the boys met several other boys that were their age. The twins attended classes each day, but my oldest son was not allowed to attend the classes because Mohamed did not have up-to-date papers on him. Therefore he spent all of those five months alone during the days as his brothers attended classes.

Each day the boys would rise early for morning prayers; five times a day they would pray. They would be beaten if they were late; however, each time they would go for prayers they would call on the name of Jesus to come and rescue them. They did this every day for more than six months. Then the Lord began to encourage them through dreams. One boy recalls dreaming that he was in a very deep pit, and at the bottom of that pit was a dragon standing in control over him. He was terrified, but then a mighty angel, tall and bright, entered into the pit, lifted his mighty sword high, slew the dragon, and helped him to escape. This gave him faith that God had heard their prayers and that He would come to their rescue.

Mohamed's father began calling us from England with periodic reports on how the boys were doing in India. Apparently, they were not doing too well. They were hot, restless, and uncomfortable and had grown very homesick. They cried often for me. They wanted to return to Saudi Arabia to be with the rest of the family.

Beyond the Veil of Darkness

I was quite surprised to hear this coming from my father-in-law, considering that he was the one financially responsible for their stay in India. I had prayed and asked God to let the family in India get tired of the boys and find them too exhausting to care for. After all, it was not easy to take care of someone else's children, especially for so long a time. I learned from my father-in-law that the Lord was doing just that to answer my prayers. The family constantly complained and fussed about having the additional responsibility of three boys. They frequently called Mohamed's father in England and pressured him to tell Mohamed to return to India and get his sons.

Recognizing that his father was under constant pressure from other members of the family, Mohamed reluctantly booked a flight and traveled to India to "check out the situation." He left in the early part of May 1990; four days later, he called from Bombay, and I was able to speak very briefly with my three sons. It was hard to control the tremor in my voice; I wanted to make the best of this short conversation. What a thrill it was to hear their voices again.

The news that Mohamed gave me was not good. There were problems with the boys' visas, which needed to be renewed in Bombay. Mohamed said that for days he waited outside the British embassy in steamy hot weather in a long line that stretched into the filthy streets of Bombay, hoping to have the matter rectified. For several days the work day ended and the doors closed before he could get inside. The only thing I could do was to pray. I remained very hopeful that God, who had answered all our prayers up to this time, would again come through for us in this situation.

After three weeks of anxiety and prayer, the doorbell rang on June 3, just as the girls and I were finishing breakfast. Imagine my delight when I opened the door to find my three sons and husband standing there. It was a dream come true. I threw my arms around them and embraced them. They were happy to see me and headed straight to their sisters' room to embrace them and inquire about their latest toys. As they chatted and shared and talked some more, I felt my nest fill again. The silence of the home was broken. The chatter was like the sweetest music to my ears. The family was once again united—a symbol that God ultimately was in control—and I thanked Him for hearing and answering my prayers.

Joy filled my heart and flooded my soul as I prepared my sons' favorite meal—spaghetti—that evening. I watched as they devoured the meal. It was such a joy to have them home again.

The boys were in good spirits, but physically, they were in pretty bad shape. They looked rather thin, and their stomachs were slightly distended. There were dry patches on their faces and other parts of their body; they appeared to be dehydrated. Their fingernails were black and their feet hardened and cracked from wearing sandals for so long. Their bodies were covered with insect bites; they looked like war veterans. The clothing on their backs and in their suitcases bore the telltale blood stains from the insect bites. My oldest son had a very deep wound on his foot; it was filled with dirt. His skin had become so dry and hard that it was cracked in places. As I set them in a bath of nice, warm water with an antiseptic solution to clean and soothe their wounds, it was readily apparent how physically and mentally exhausted they were.

I noticed that their hair was filled with lice. They laughed at each other as they talked about who had the most lice. I could tell that they had found a way to cope with the many discomforts they had endured. What a great God we serve!

I decided that the best way to get rid of the lice problem was to shave their heads, and I bought a special shampoo to kill the lice. We had a good laugh at their bald heads. All the while, Mohamed was nonchalant; he just sat and watched television as I fussed over the boys, cleaning them up and trying to make them comfortable once again.

Oh, how my heart rejoiced that night as I retired to bed. I slept soundly, knowing that all my children were under my roof. There was peace and comfort in my heart. Anna called my family in England to let them know that the boys were back home. They rejoiced at this news.

Now that my family and I were all together, my church families in England and the United States began to fast and pray that God would release me and the children from Saudi Arabia. I prayed and asked God that I would be able to leave with dignity, not looking over my shoulder and not running from the enemy. I reminded the Lord that I had come to this country on a mission for Him. "You sent me here, Lord; now You please take me out," I pleaded.

Over the next several days, Mohamed's anger and appearance of deep contemplation concerned me. One could only imagine how defeated he must have felt. After all, he had worked very hard to try to convert me to Islam, and nothing seemed to work. His sense of defeat must have been particularly intense when he was forced by circumstances to bring the boys back home. I continued to pray for our quick release as I contemplated what Mohamed might do next.

chapter 16

Just Let Me Be Their Mother

A few weeks after the boys were back home, Mohamed informed me that he was in the process of seriously looking for a second wife. When I heard this, I immediately prayed for an extra dispensation of strength and courage. I had read somewhere that each trial always prepares you for the next and that the next is always bigger than the previous one, but somehow I felt ill-prepared for this. Mohamed went on to assure me that I would always be the first wife, and the other woman would be the second wife. I can't honestly say that it came as any assurance to me. I asked him if he was considering making his Indian friend his second wife. He said that he was not interested in her anymore but that he would be conducting interviews to find a wife.

One evening some time after his announcement we were visiting in the home of one of his friends for dinner. His friend's wife confided that Mohamed had asked her husband to keep an eye out for a prospective wife for him. She told me that although in Islam the women accepted their husbands' rights to have up to four wives at one time, it was still the last thing that even the native women wanted. She was herself a Muslim but empathized with me for what I was going through. She found it difficult to understand why Mohamed was treating me the way he was and told me that he was not a good Muslim, judging from the way he was behaving.

God strengthened me to face the trials as He had always done in the past, and He directed my thoughts to the lessons that I needed to learn from my experiences. I began to understand the wisdom in the Bible's counsel to not be unequally yoked with unbelievers. I reflected over my life and wished that I had obeyed my parents and the Word of God. The consequences of bad decisions have a deleterious effect that could, and often do, last a life-time. I had no one to blame but myself.

The accuser of the brethren worked on my guilt and mistakes of the past, reminding me that I was deserving of everything that was happening to me. But I was able to say, "Truly I am deserving of everything, but because Christ died for me; He has set me free from sin and death; and even though I may have to face these consequences of my past rejection of Christ, now that I know Him, I have the hope of overcoming and experiencing His forgiveness and His power to save. So, yes, I am a sinner saved by grace."

Mohamed continued to talk of a new wife. Islamic custom dictates that all wives be treated equally with the same provisions. He shared that his second wife would have to live with us until he could get an apartment for her. It surprised me how comfortable he was just sitting and talking to me about his plans to remarry, as though I was just a casual observer or that I was not even human and had no feeling. What surprised me more was how the Lord was with me as I sat and talked with him and encouraged him in his despair. I knew it had to be the Spirit of God speaking through me. He gave me the courage to face this situation. I told God that whatever He wanted me to be, I would be. I gave myself in complete surrender to Him and said, "Lord, if You want me to stay, I will stay. There is no better or safer place to be than in Your will." I loved the Lord so much and was willing to do anything He commanded. I no longer doubted Him or the plans He had for me. I said, "Lord, if You would have me to be a witness to this new wife, then I will be Your vessel through whom Your Holy Spirit will shine."

After this commitment, I received a calm assurance from God that I would be able to live in whatever circumstances I would be placed in from that point onward.

As Mohamed observed the love and affection the children and I shared, he became very jealous. He knew we had something very special going on. Mohamed started threatening again to send me away and to have me escorted on an airplane back to England because my Christian influence would affect the upbringing of the children. Panic came over me, and I begged and pleaded with him to let me stay. Not that I wanted to stay in Saudi Arabia, but I could not bear another separation from any of the children. I promised him that I would not have worship with the children any more, and that I would not interfere with his Islamic teaching. I made that promise because God had already prepared me for this situation through the pages of inspiration dealing with the influence of the Christian mother in the home. The following passage from the book *The Adventist Home* had caught my attention.

> Next to God, the mother's power for good is the strongest known on earth.
>
> The mother's influence is an unceasing influence....
>
> When her influence is for truth, for virtue, when she is guided by divine wisdom, what a power for Christ will be her life! Her influence will reach on through time into eternity. What a thought is this—that the mother's looks and words and actions bear fruit in eternity, and the salvation or ruin of many will be the result of her influence!
>
> Little does the mother realize that her influence in the judicious training of her children reaches with such power through the vicissitudes of this life, stretching forward into the future, immortal life. To fashion a character after the heavenly Model requires much faithful, earnest, persevering labor; but it will pay, for God is a rewarder of all well-directed labor in securing the salvation of souls.
>
> The tenderest earthly tie is that between the mother and her child. The child is more readily impressed by the life and

example of the mother than by that of the father, for a stronger and more tender bond of union unites them. —*The Adventist Home*, 240.

This passage assured me that my influence as a Christian mother was more powerful than any other force on this earth. So, no matter what the outcome, as long as I sat at the feet of Jesus and received His influence in my life, it would have the same effect as worshiping with the children and teaching them about Christ. I realized that God was not only going to save my children, but He would also save me in the process.

Victory was mine! I remembered Moses' mother and how her influence was of a power to save not only Moses but also the whole nation of Israel. I told Mohamed that I just wanted to be the children's mother. "Just let me be their mother, care for them, and feed them. That's all I want to be," I implored. I fell on my knees and begged the Lord to please set us free, but only if it was His will.

chapter 17

Mission Accomplished

Anxiety was building as I wondered what would happen next. My prayers for an army to come and rescue me and the children continued with more intensity. I learned to live one day at a time while waiting for divine intervention.

While the days lingered on, I found comfort in songs that lifted my heart to heaven. One morning I awoke to the voices of angels singing to me, strengthening me, and watering my soul with music. It was a song of hope and joy. The sweet, melodious voices of the heavenly choir once again encouraged me. The thought that God would minister to my personal needs in such a singular way brought sweet assurance that He would never leave me, no matter how dark the night.

One evening Mohamed returned from work with the news that Saddam Hussein had invaded Kuwait. This action was very unsettling in the Middle East. Immediately, my thoughts reflected on my prayers for an army to rescue me.

Strange as it may seem, this turn of events gave me more hope. I felt that my faith was about to be rewarded with the reality of a rescue. It was as if God was saying, "You have been tried and tested, and now I am about to set you free. Be still and know that I am God."

Many Westerners were leaving the country in fear for their lives and of an imminent war. I asked Mohamed if we could leave too. His answer was No. Still, I believed that the hand of God would become evident in the events that were taking place on a worldwide scale. I sensed that He would use these circumstances to bring about an answer to my prayer.

I was mindful of the parable of the ninety-nine sheep that were left in the fold by the shepherd as He went in search of the one lost sheep. I knew that God would empty all of heaven to rescue one lost child; and I was that one in the Middle East, in the abyss of darkness, crying for the angel of light to rescue me. Would God disappoint me?

Several weeks went by. My family called from England and told me that they were praying and fasting and collecting money for our airfare out of Saudi Arabia. These were all acts of faith, because there was no guarantee that Mohamed would change his mind and let us leave.

On several occasions I spoke to Anna to let her know what was going on. She remained in contact with my family to keep them apprised of the situation. Meanwhile, just the thought that my church family was praying for our deliverance gave me the spiritual boost I needed.

I visited with Anna and left her my Bible and other Christian literature to read. There was no point in leaving the country with them when they were so difficult to get through customs. She was very happy to receive them. We prayed together, and she promised she would read them. God was moving. I could feel the victory close at hand.

But Mohamed's heart was as hard as that of Pharaoh of old, who refused to let Israel go despite Moses' pleas. I felt like a prisoner of war. I found myself beginning to get panicky and anxious at times. The Lord quieted my spirit and helped me to rest while He worked. I felt sapped of energy; there was no more fight left in me. It was all left up to the Lord at this point. I was so tired of agonizing with the Lord, but in my weakness I was assured that He was carrying me over the victory line.

More than a year had passed by since we had arrived in Saudi Arabia. It seemed like a lifetime. I stopped to consider all that we had gone through since we had been here. As I gazed over the past year and read through my diary of events, I found myself drained and completely resting in Jesus. As I reflected over all that had taken place, I realized that I would not have made it this far without the Word of God by my side, to instruct me and guide me, and the writings of favorite Christian authors to teach me life skills necessary for my growth as a child of God. God's wonderful power was even more clear and distinguishable now. It came to my realization that I had experienced a mini end-time conflict where we must stand for our faith.

Scripture assures us that we must do all we can to stand putting our full trust in God and having on His full armor. I had been severely tested for my faith in Jesus Christ. The things that I had cherished most were all removed from me: my basic human rights, justice, and freedom—even my children. I realized that the only thing that I could say I really owned was the power of choice, and I chose Christ above all that I cherished. I had died to self, not through anything that I did but through Christ working in me. Now I could see the enormity of sin and the suffering, great suffering, that it caused. I understood more clearly why Christ had to die.

Do we really know what we are asking when we ask God to see us through into the kingdom?

Not at all, for you see, we are asking God to take us through the road that is tailor-made for us, and we must trust Him to do so. The path He leads you down may not be the path you would have chosen—you might have a rough journey into the kingdom. We were never promised that the road would be smooth, but we are promised that Jesus will never leave us nor forsake us. God will remove every idol, whatever it may be, whatever gives you a false sense of security, every besetting, sinful trait of character, until all is wiped clean.

I was of no use to my children when they were gone; I couldn't bathe them, dress them, feed them, or even embrace them. I had to depend on a Power greater than myself to do all that I could not. Jesus is the caretaker over all our earthly transactions, so why don't we learn now in this time of peace to let go and trust in God? Why do we have to wait for calamity to come to force us to trust Him? It has been said that many will learn the skill of trusting during the terrible conflicts on earth just before Jesus comes.

But who will stand today and in those last days before Jesus comes? Many will be allowed to fall asleep in Jesus to spare them the trials of living through the last and final days. Judging from the pain that I felt in my trials, I cannot imagine anything worse, but we cannot begin to imagine what it will be like. So we need to obey God's commands now and not hesitate, if we can learn to deny self and not always do those things that are comfortable for us and that which makes us feel good—always wanting to be the first and the best.

Too many of God's children live to gratify self. In self there is no victory. We dress the way we want, eat the way we want, and go the places we want, and we think that God doesn't mind because He loves us. Self is the greatest enemy that we as Christians have to fight against. If we could just conquer our selfish desires and leave out those things that are not edifying to us morally, that degenerate us physically, and that ruin us spiritually—if we would begin to do that now when all is apparently well in our lives, trusting in God's Word, it will strengthen us for the time when test and trial come our way. All of us will go through test and trial, so why not prepare now?

So many who would be saints will fail because they never learned the discipline of self-denial. They will give in to hunger and other felt needs; others will sell their own children. In the days of trial just before the fall of Jerusalem, mothers even cooked and ate their own children. We like to think that we are in control of everything and that when those times come, we will deny self and do this or that. But many who have this confidence will be very surprised at how they might respond in severe trials.

The power of making a good choice in trying times is based upon having a sound mind, strong reasoning powers, and a healthy intellect. God has given us instruction how to bring this about through healthful living and study of Scripture. Since the mind and the body are in such close connection with one another, it matters a great deal what we eat and drink and what we do with our bodies—getting enough sleep, water, sunshine, and exercise. As we walk through the hospitals, we see many sick people.

Mission Accomplished

If we were to trace back the treatment of their bodies, we would see the effects of their diets on most of the illnesses. God has set rules for His children so they can live longer and be His witnesses. It's very difficult for people to believe that simple things such as one's diet and care for the human machinery will be major, deciding factors when it comes to making choices for life or death. Without a sound mind and body, we lessen our chances for being victorious.

Our thoughts must be brought under the control of the Holy Spirit. We must guard the things we look at and the things we hear. We should do all we can to live up to all that we know. God deals with us right where we are. His blood shed on Calvary is plenty enough to cover every sinful person who walks with Him, living up to the truth He reveals.

Don't let anyone tell you that diet is not important. I had no idea what living up to all the light I had known would do for me in a time of severe pressure and torment and pain. That's why we must not question God on His commands for us as a people. Just fall in love with Jesus and trust and obey Him even when you don't understand. We have become a people of knowledge and intellect. We question everything; we reason away the simple commands that a baby can understand so we can have our own way. We see a "Thus saith the Lord," but we question it. God knew what He was saying when He said we must be as little children to enter into the kingdom. Children are so vulnerable, they understand simple commands. God only expects us to live up to what we know, not denying what He says is best for us but moving in faith, denying ourselves, and trusting in His leading. This is how we put on the armor of God. Piece by piece, as Ephesians 6:11-17 says.

So as I contemplated how God had led me in the past and searched myself to be sure that I was living up to what He had revealed to me, I realized that only when I had done this could I stand on His promises and demand my freedom from all of this oppression. Now it was time for God to act. It was time for me to sit back and rest on His word.

I am a living witness that when you do all you can to stand, when you live up to the light God sheds on your path, you can depend on Him to do the rest.

chapter 18

Deliverance

A couple more weeks went by, and still Mohamed refused to sign the papers that would allow us to leave. I felt impressed to pray and ask the Lord to work this one more miracle. One evening Mohamed returned from work looking very forlorn and worried. He explained that his job was folding and that the company was in the midst of financial struggles. Stress and fear was written all over his face.

With a war on the horizon and our own financial challenges, this was the worst time for something like this to happen. Mohamed was already in a lot of debt, and he was hoping to enroll the children in school in Saudi Arabia for the first time. This would be very costly because he had hoped to enroll them in either the British or the American school. In addition, our half-yearly rent was due.

Mohamed's back was against the wall, and he could see no way out. His job offered him a bachelor's apartment, and his employer advised him that it would be best to send his family home for now. Mohamed was distressed, but I could see the power of God working on our behalf. There was nothing he could do, and he knew it. He slumped on the couch, defeat and bewilderment written on his face.

Victory for me was assured as he began to relinquish his hold on us, but I had to be careful not to gloat over Mohamed's failure. In some ways, my heart was saddened to see him finally giving up the fight due to no choice of his own. But he could see that our family unit was being destroyed. I comforted him and encouraged him, because I realized that we are all sinners. We all make mistakes. What Mohamed had done, he had done out of misguided love for his children. My heart had so much sympathy for him; I knew it had to be God's loving sympathy toward His wayward children being manifested in me toward Mohamed.

Mohamed gave me exact instructions on how we should conduct ourselves when we returned to England. He instructed me to put the children in Islamic schools and to cover myself like a Muslim woman. I could hear panic and desperation in his voice as he looked at his family, knowing he had probably lost them forever. At this point I thought that I would be jumping for joy, laughing in his face, and boasting over whose God is the biggest and greatest. Instead, I cried for the pain and the confusion he was feeling. I imagined the pain he was going to go through, very similar to that which I had been going through. I wouldn't wish it on my worst enemy. When God says "Vengeance is mine," we should step aside and leave the consequences in His hands. It is a dangerous thing to be an obstacle in the way of the children of God. We are the apple of His eye, and He will come to our aid. Those who fall into the hands of God without being covered by His grace will certainly live to regret all that they have done.

Mohamed wondered aloud where we would get the money for air tickets for the children and me to leave the country. He didn't know that my family had already raised the money and purchased the tickets, and the tickets for the six of us were at the Air Egypt office waiting to be picked up at our convenience. When I told him that, he looked amazed, and he had no choice but to accept them. This was a hard thing for a proud man like Mohamed to do. It made me realize that "Pride goeth before destruction, and an haughty spirit before a fall," as the Bible says in Proverbs 16:18.

Mohamed began to process our exit visas, and for the first time since we arrived in Saudi Arabia, I saw our passports. He had kept them in his office at work. Reservations were made on Air Egypt for August 15, 1990.

The last few days were filled with excitement and anxiety as Mohamed kept changing his mind about whether to let us leave or not. It was very stressful, but I kept my faith in God, knowing that everything was under His control. August 15 finally came; our suitcases were packed, and we were ready to leave. The children and I were very excited, but I had instructed the children not to appear too happy about leaving, because we were leaving their father behind.

Mohamed drove us to the airport, giving instructions all along the way. When we arrived, my heart was pounding in my chest. The children and I were very nervous, expecting Mohamed to change his mind at any time and return us home. I kept praying, "Lord, please let us go."

The check-in line was very long, giving Mohamed plenty of time to change his mind if he wished. When it was finally our turn at the desk, I wondered if he would just check me in and take the children back home. I had to trust God, for truly this was His plan in operation. It could have happened no other way. God was the one checking us out of the country, not Mohamed. When we reached the metal detectors, Mohamed could go no farther. One by one we went through. We waved and began walking toward the gate, leaving him in the distance. We turned once again and saw his face in the far distance. We waved again, our last good-byes.

Once aboard the aircraft, I looked out of the window and saw the man I had married standing in the airport terminal looking down at the airplane. He looked so alone. I wondered what he was thinking, what kind of thoughts were racing through his mind. He had put up a good fight. But the battle he had sought to win was against a Power infinitely greater than him. And there he was, bereft of everything he had sought to win in his own might. I, on the other hand, was richer for my experiences. I had my children and a stronger faith in God's providential leading. Sure, times were tough. But I had come with Christ, and I was leaving with Christ. Mission accomplished.

chapter 19

Free at Last

Sitting aboard the Air Egypt jumbo jet, we were ready for the flight to England to see relatives and friends, with a stopover in Cairo. Chairs in the upright position, seat belts fastened, ready for takeoff. *Something must be wrong,* I thought. This procedure usually takes only a few minutes before the door is closed and the plane is in the air. But the door was still open, and we were still on the ground.

Oh no! Mohamed could not have changed his mind again! Knowing Mohamed, I was fully aware that he could. *He wouldn't drive us all the way here, have us board the plane, and then stop the flight from taking off, would he?* But I knew that Mohamed was capable of doing almost anything and going to almost any extreme to accomplish his purpose. These and other thoughts raced through my mind as the plane sat on the runway and the children and I waited with bated breath. I fully expected the officials to board the plane at any time and order the children or all of us off the plane.

The minutes ticked by slowly. Finally, after an hour, I saw the door to the aircraft close and heard the engines revving up. The children looked at me, and I looked at their hesitant, anxious faces. The plane taxied down the runway, building up speed, faster, faster, faster. As it lifted off the ground, I could finally lean back as my taut muscles began to relax ever so slowly. I could not relax completely, fearing that at any moment during the flight, the plane would be summoned to return to Saudi Arabia.

As we landed in Cairo, it seemed as if the Lord had angels stationed everywhere to ensure our safety and to escort us to the hotel where we would spend the night before boarding the flight to England. I was dressed in my Muslim attire, as this was a safe way for me to travel in the Middle East with my children.

That night we worshiped the Lord in spirit and in truth. We sang praises to Him together for the first time in a long time. We prayed, thanked the Lord, had a hot meal, and retired for the night. We arose early the next morning, had our devotions, and went for breakfast. Then we took the airport taxi to continue our flight to England.

Almost the whole family was at the airport to meet us when we got to England—everybody but my mother. They wanted to surprise her. What joy was on their faces! We embraced each other and cried for joy. As we traveled from the airport, I looked at the green hills of England and praised God for freedom. Free at last!

Mother was surprised and overjoyed to see us. We stood in a circle, held hands, and praised God for His goodness and for sparing our lives. Joy spread across the Atlantic Ocean as my church family in the United States got the news of our release.

I called Mohamed to let him know that we had arrived safely. To my surprise, he asked us to return to Saudi Arabia because his job had been reinstated and he had received a promotion and a raise in salary. It sounded like a good offer, so I consulted the Lord to see what His will was. I believe that, even in what seems obvious, we must always seek the will of God. As I searched the Scriptures for an answer, the Lord led me to Galatians 5:1, which said, "Stand fast therefore in the liberty wherewith Christ hath made us free, and be not entangled again with the yoke of bondage."

That said it all! There was my answer. I did not question God. He spoke clearly, and I was so relieved and overjoyed to know that I would be free from bondage. Mohamed was very disappointed and pleaded for us to return, but I realized that those whom Christ has set free are free indeed (John 8:36).

Free at Last

For weeks after that I lived in fear. Mohamed was very angry and threatened to take the children back. After all Christ had done for me, I was still overwhelmed with doubt. I was afraid that Mohamed's spies and family members would see the children going to church. I made sure that they went to Islamic schools in the evening to continue learning the Quran. It's amazing how controlling fear can be. Mohamed had warned me that if I did not comply with his wishes for the children's education, he would send people to abduct the children, and I believed him.

It took awhile for me to realize that fear did not come from God and that I could not continue my life in that way. I went from being fearful to being very bold. I took the bold step of filing for a complete separation from him by way of a divorce. I felt that I had to do it, and I was prepared to live the rest of my life without him and to rear my children alone.

Divorce is a great controversy in our churches today. Some believe we should stay in marriages for better or for worse. But going through the worst does not mean one partner having a rough time in the marriage and being taken advantage of by the other. It simply means going through bad times together, supporting and loving each other through it all and sharing in those sad times.

God does not like divorce, even though He made a way out for those who would suffer and live a bitter life. God has given us provisions to live in an unequal union, but it requires constant prayer, self-denial, and His abundant grace. The Christian life is hard enough without bringing on ourselves burdens that God never ordained for us. That's why we are warned not to be unequally yoked in marriage. Many of us live each day in a cloud of gloom with the partners we have chosen for ourselves.

To the converted one in the marriage, God's grace is sufficient—you can choose joy. The fruit of the spirit is yours for the asking. Study the Word of God. By beholding you will become changed. You will manifest the fruit of the Spirit. Christ living in you will make you loving, patient, and kind. I know of married couples who are together but long for the unconverted partner to know Jesus. Yet at the same time they have a good working relationship with each other. We cannot force our partners to believe, but we can represent Christ. Christ is the power that draws. Jesus said "And I, if I be lifted up from the earth, will draw all men unto me" (John 12:32). God has made it possible for us to forgive our partners, even if he or she commits adultery. The marriage bed being defiled is the only reason God has given for divorce with the possibility for remarriage. But it's best if we can work out marital problems, including adultery, with prayer and good Christian counseling.

If it were only adultery I had to contend with, I believe God would have given me the grace to remain in my marriage. But when the unconverted partner becomes an obstacle in the way of your relationship with God in addition to living an adulterous life, then God will intercede. He will not have you mocked. And so with prayerful steps my divorce proceeded.

Mohamed fought the divorce all the way. It was very painful. He accused me of being a member of a cult and a Satan worshiper. He offered the children a beautiful home with a swimming pool, servants, and a good education in Saudi schools.

After eight months of court battle, primarily over the custody issue, I was granted full and complete custody of all five children. I was overjoyed and filled with gratitude to God. The children started to attend school in England, where we settled in a lovely home. We even managed to buy a car, thanks to loving church members who cared enough to help us out financially. We set up visitation for Mohamed, but he was not allowed to be alone with the children. Mohamed continues to live in Saudi Arabia. We always pray that Mohamed will give his life to the Lord, and we believe that, as long as the door of mercy is open, there will always be a chance for him to come to Christ. Therefore, we continue a courteous relationship toward him.

On one of his visits, my prayer for him was that he would see Jesus in us and come to know Christ's sacrifice for him.

An incident soon occurred that I believe was an answer to that prayer.

chapter 20

Christ's Power Over Evil

Jeffrey, my brother, was a martial arts expert. At about the time I returned from Saudi Arabia, he was going though a very difficult phase in his life. For a long time drugs and alcohol dominated his life.

His behavior was so strange at times that one visiting pastor diagnosed him as being demon-possessed. We had thought that for a long time. He was very much acquainted with the witches and warlocks in the area and was known to attend many of their coven meetings. He had even told us that he had witnessed many awful, supernatural sights during some of the rituals.

Jeffrey seemed to possess supernatural demonic power. He was truly evil, and it was quite frightening to be around him when he was drinking or using drugs. Satan seemed to be in complete control of him. His actions were unpredictable. Finally, Jeffrey came to realize that he needed release from the demons that were holding him captive.

One evening, the local minister, along with several members, visited Jeffrey at his home. The minister proceeded to pray in every room of the house, casting out demons from every corner. With that completed, the church members encircled Jeffrey, and the minister continued to call out the names of demons that were supposedly in control of Jeffrey. With every name came a deep groan and a wrestling in his body as the spirits fought to remain in control. There were shrill shrieks and deep penetrating groans—voices that were not Jeffrey's. His body writhed as if in agony. When the last demon was called out, Jeffrey fell to the ground as if lifeless, frothing at the mouth as the members began to sing "Power in the Blood."

At the end of this episode, Jeffrey sprang to his feet and, with outstretched arms, fell on his knees, crying and weeping and praising God for his freedom from the bondage of the demons. This was a wonderful moment; all who were present were deeply affected by this experience. Truly the power of Christ was triumphant over the powers of evil.

Jeffrey lived a clean and upright life for four years. He was a new person. He loved his wife once again and treated her with love and respect. He was a loving and devoted father to his two children. The Lord began to use Jeffrey. He once again was the priest in his home, leading out in family worship. His diet changed, and he began to eat only wholesome foods.

His ministry extended from the home into the church community. He had a unique relationship with the children in the church. He became quite a hero to them. He served as a deacon in his church. His former friends and drinking buddies were completely amazed at the dramatic change that had taken place in Jeffrey's life. They often tried to tempt him with alcohol and drugs, but he showed no desire to get involved and stood as a marvelous example of Christ's overwhelming victory over sin.

But the devil wasn't through with him. One day, as a result of being provoked on the job, he grabbed a co-worker, and this led to his dismissal from the job. When the matter came to the attention of the church, he was removed from his post as a deacon. One thing led to another, and before long his life began to spiral downward. He began again to use his favorite salad dressing that had wine as one of the ingredients. This whetted his taste for more alcohol in larger doses. In the meantime, his search for a job was fruitless, leading him to a sense of hopelessness and rejection. Jeffrey had a lot of time on his hands; he became more and more restless and frustrated. Nothing seemed to be going right for him, and he continued to attempt to drown out his problems with alcohol. He especially felt rejected by his church family.

I was very concerned about my brother's mental and spiritual health. I tried my best to encourage him—all the while praying that somehow he would experience a breakthrough in what seemed like a dark night of despair.

One night Jeff dreamed that he answered a knock at his door only to find a cute little kitten waiting to enter. "No, Jeff," I warned in the dream, "don't let him in." But Jeff replied, "It's only one little kitten. He's cute and hungry." He took pity on the kitten and opened the door wider. Suddenly a rush of thousands of kittens overran Jeffrey and entered the house. It reminded me of the Scripture that tells us that when Satan leaves a vessel, he returns to check on it to see whether it is occupied or left vacant. If he finds it vacant, he will rush in to occupy it once again but with a greater number of demons than ever before.

Jeffrey was concerned, but his concern did not curb his spiritual slide. He began to grow more careless about studying the Word of God, and his prayer life was virtually dead. He visited his old friends with the intention of witnessing to them, but he was only placing himself in the path of temptation, and the old habits of drinking, smoking, and using drugs returned. Instead of drinking from the streams of life that never run dry, he was using whiskey and other alcoholic drinks in an attempt to drown out his problems. Satan was once again taking control of my brother.

Now, Jeffrey had been especially disturbed about my experiences in Saudi Arabia. I did not realize how hurt he was and neither did anyone else. He never gave his angry feelings over to the Lord. Anger was allowed to fester in his heart, and he became obsessed with thoughts of repaying Mohamed for what he had put me through.

chapter 21

What Love!

One time when Mohamed came to visit, Jeffery made plans with demonic agencies to kill him. For a period of about two weeks prior to Mohamed's visit, Jeff was awakened every night by demons who would tell him to drink a bottle of whiskey, get his sword, and go and kill Mohamed.

The children were happy to see their father. In addition to Mohamed, my girlfriend and her two sons who were friends of my boys were also visiting us. Suddenly, there was a very loud knock at the door. I opened it to find Jeff staggering drunk. He pushed past me into the living room where Mohamed was sitting in a chair by the door. Immediately the atmosphere changed from laughter to darkness and fear as, with hatred in his eyes, Jeffrey looked at Mohamed and began to beat him with heavy blows. Jeffrey was a big man and very strong.

My girlfriend grabbed the children and took them upstairs to pray. She returned to see what she could do to help. By this time, Mohamed was in a state of shock and seemed very helpless. He managed to stand to his feet, dazed, but Jeff was relentless in his attacks. My friend and I screamed for Jeff to stop. We tried to restrain him, but he was too strong for us. He threw us aside and cried out in a demonic voice that Mohamed would have to die for what he had done to me in Saudi Arabia. I pleaded for him to spare Mohamed's life, but my pleas were falling on deaf ears. It was a frightening scene.

The break we needed came when Jeff ran out to his car to get his sword. He had been driving around with it in the hope of seeing Mohamed and chopping him to bits. I took the opportunity to flick open the back window and order Mohamed to jump through and escape. Mohamed was slow at grasping my orders; he was somewhat disoriented from the blows, and his mouth was bleeding.

As he approached the window, Jeff burst into the room again with the presence of evil before and behind him. Even his skin color had changed to a grayish tone; he was accompanied with a supernatural power of darkness. I knew that I was no longer contending with Jeff, my brother, but with demons. I no longer pleaded for Jeff to spare Mohamed's life; I called on the name of Jesus to rebuke the evil presence that was in my home. "Satan, in the name of Jesus I command you to leave this place!"

My girlfriend stood far back as she prayed and looked on in horror as Jeff raised his sword, cutting the dining table; then he raised it again and cursed, this time slicing off a leg on one of the dining room chairs. Then he began to describe how he was going to chop Mohamed up. He stood and went into a kind of trance as he described cutting off Mohamed's arms from the shoulders and leaving his head until last.

At that point, the fear left me, and I jumped and stood in front of the sword. It was razor sharp. I took hold of the long blade. Jeff looked at me, and our eyes met. I said, while praying for protection from the demons, "I am not talking to Jeff but to the demon within him. In the name of Jesus, leave my brother's body! Leave now!" I held on tightly to the sword. Jeff pleaded with me to let go of it, but I told him that I could not, and that if he pulled the sword I would lose all of my fingers.

I continued to stand between Mohamed and the sword. Jeff was afraid of hurting me. I kept shouting for Mohamed to escape out the window. "Run, run!" I screamed. Mohamed was so confused he was afraid to run. All of a sudden I heard myself pleading for Jeff to take my life instead of Mohamed's. "Kill me, kill me!" I implored. "Don't kill Mohamed! Please

What Love!

Jeff, don't do it! I'll die for him!"

At this point, Mohamed started for the window. Everything seemed to be happening in slow motion. Jeff was getting to the point where he wanted to make a quick end of this episode. Somehow the sword was freed, so I grabbed Jeff from behind with all the strength I had. Locking my hands in front of him to keep his arms down, I was able to give Mohamed the few extra seconds he needed to get out of the window. The window crashed down on Mohamed as he fought to get out quickly. Just then Jeff broke loose and swung the sword in anger. But Mohamed broke free just in the nick of time and ran around the backyard and out into the front of the house.

Jeff had covered all bases in an effort to prevent Mohamed from escaping. He had previously slashed the tires on his car and stationed two other men outside to catch him if he tried to run away. However, Mohamed managed to slip by the two men as he fled. He ran into the dark fields nearby, blood dripping everywhere from injuries he had suffered while getting out through the window.

Jeff ran outside and rebuked the men who had failed him. Then he jumped into his car in an effort to catch Mohamed, but the car would not start; the battery was dead. This gave Mohamed another opportunity to get out of sight.

No matter what Jeff did, he was thwarted in his attempt to bring further harm to Mohamed. He tried desperately to push the car to start, but it was to no avail; God had restrained him. He sank to the ground and, looking up at the dark sky, cried out in anger, "Master, I failed you. I'm sorry I failed you." It was a sad scene as Jeff lamented, apologizing to Satan for failing to carry out the mandate to destroy another human being.

I grabbed Jeff and continued to hold him while he cursed and rebuked his helpers; they were obviously afraid of him. With all the strength I could muster, I held onto my brother and called down rebukes on Satan.

By this time the neighbors had called the police. When they finally came, they asked if I wanted to press charges. I refused, telling them that it was only a family disagreement, so they left.

After a little while longer, the car started, and Jeff, along with his two friends, took off to resume their search for Mohamed. I prayed for his safety and called people who might have seen him, to see if I could locate him to let him know that Jeff was still looking for him. Later, my sister called to say that he was in the emergency room of the hospital, having his wounds cared for. He had suffered cuts and bruises and had to have stitches in his hand.

Several hours later I was still overwhelmed by the events that had occurred. It was almost impossible to rest. In the early hours of the next day, I found Jeff at a friend's house. I walked in, sat down, and held his hands. The effects of the alcohol were wearing off. He looked up at me with bloodshot eyes, smiled weakly, and said, "Esmie, you have some power with you." He went on to tell me that when he entered into my home, he felt a great deal of power leave him. Christ had arrested him at the door.

He said that he was trying so hard to hurt Mohamed, but every blow felt as if it was done in slow motion with hardly any effect. He was amazed at how I was able to restrain him. He looked at me again and said, "You have some power! Yes, you have the power!"

"Yes, Jeff," I replied. "The power of Christ is available to us whenever we need it."

"Every time you called on the name of Jesus, I became weaker and weaker until I could not lift my arms," he said. "I was struggling to, but I just couldn't do it." He then testified of the great victorious power of Christ over Satan. Even the demons must confess that Jesus is Lord.

What a victory, what a joy we have in Christ! Satan cannot conquer the weakest child of God who depends on divine strength. I hugged my brother, said goodbye, and went home to assure the children that all was going to be fine and that their father was all right.

That night I reflected on how much in control God truly was. He had answered my prayers. Mohamed saw a wonderful manifestation of Christ's love. He saw an enactment of the plan of salvation, that even though we are sinners Christ still loves us. He came and stood between the blade of death and us. He is our Mediator and Advocate, even though we are so unloving, unlovely, and sinful. He covers us unconditionally with His love. He pleads every day, "Father, My blood, My blood was shed for this sinner."

God had done something through me that I was so unworthy of. His love, His sacrifice was acted out through me in such an awful moment. What an awesome God!

The next morning, I visited Mohamed at his father's store. He was still a little shaken. He was never one for communicating, and he never shared his thoughts with me about what had taken place. However, I believe that he will always remember the strange scene of me pleading for my death rather than his, a symbol of what Christ had already done on our behalf. "Greater love hath no man than this, that a man lay down his life for his friends" (John 15:13).

I witnessed a marvelous change come over Mohamed. That day he was brave enough to visit Jeff. They greeted each other with open arms, embracing one another. Somehow, without a word spoken, there was an understanding between them.

Jeff offered Mohamed a meal. They ate, discussed their hurts, cried, embraced again, and separated. For a moment at least, Mohamed was a new person.

chapter 22

Waiting on the Lord

Mohamed decided that he would take a Muslim wife who could better fit into his lifestyle. He wanted to bring peace to his family by abiding by their rules at last, so he allowed his parents to arrange a marriage for him.

We had been divorced for several months. Yet I hoped that God would somehow change his heart and make us whole together again. Mohamed's words had the ring of finality, and I wept at his decision and the pain my children were experiencing as result.

I wondered if I should wait for Mohamed to change his life and surrender to God. I had pretty much made up my mind not to remarry unless he remarried first. My sense of loss was so real. I began to question the Lord "Why? Why do I have to lose my husband? Did You do all that You possibly could to save him and draw him close to You? Did You? Did You, Lord?"

As I waited, the Lord spoke to me as He had always done and continues to do when I am in desperate need of hearing from Him. My God never fails. He led me to Isaiah 65:1, 2, " 'I am sought of them that asked not for me; I am found of them that sought me not: I said, Behold me, behold me, unto a nation that was not called by my name. I have spread out my hands all the day unto a rebellious people, which walketh in a way that was not good, after their own thoughts.' "

It seemed He was saying to me, "Esmie, I did all I could to present Myself to Mohamed. I used everything but force." That thought consoled me. But the sorrow was so deep, it made me wonder how the God of Israel must feel as He seemingly bends over backwards to reach His wayward children, and they would not be saved. My heart wept as I grieved for a very special lost soul, that of the father of my children.

I had to move on with my life, so I decided to go back to school and be professionally trained so that I could better support myself and my five children. The Lord showed me that He wanted me to do social work, and I was happy with that.

I had heard about a single parent program at Andrews University, located in Berrien Springs, Michigan, in the United States, to which I applied and was accepted. The difficulty came when I applied for my alien visa to be returned to me so that I would be able to return to the United States. It was a tedious process that involved a lot of paperwork and red tape. After about eleven months of serious prayer and fasting and three attempts to get my visa, I was finally granted visas for me and my British-born sons.

The children and I landed at Kennedy Airport in New York on May 3, 1992, with the intention of spending some time in Connecticut with my sisters before going on to Andrews in the fall. As we headed for Connecticut from the airport, I reflected back on how God had led me in the past. All of a sudden, I questioned if God was really leading me to Michigan and into the social work field. My heart was rapidly sinking into doubt and despair when I heard the roar of a bus passing our car. When I looked out the window, a bus emblazoned with large letters that read "ANDREWS UNIVERSITY" zoomed ahead.

What a great and wonderful God we serve! I knew that this was no coincidence. God had sent me support, encouragement, and direction at the time I desperately needed it. It seemed to me that I could hear the voice of God saying to me, "I will go before thee, and make the crooked places straight." I was assured that God certainly had a plan for me and that I must continue to trust Him. I praised God for His guidance and for the immediate attention that He always gives to me.

One month after we returned to the United States, Mohamed remarried. I was sad and discouraged. I grieved for quite some time. Then God assured me that He had plans for my life, and I needed to get busy. For six weeks I worked as a Bible worker and singing evangelist in Elmira in upstate New York. I enjoyed my freedom to witness, and to share my faith was a joyful experience. As Jeremiah said, it was like fire shut up in my bones. For too long I had had to keep quiet. After experiencing the love of God, it is difficult to keep silent. During this time, I met many wonderful people, and the church family was very generous and supportive.

Although I had been accepted at Andrews, there was some difficulty on the housing front. The director of the Genesis program, the social work program I wanted to enter, called to let me know that the program was filling up rapidly and that they were unable to provide me housing at this time. She suggested that I plan to enter the program the following school year. This suggestion did not coincide with what I felt were God's plans for me. I told her that I was following the Lord's will for me and that He had called me to enter the program at Andrews the current year, not the next.

But things were seemingly hopeless as far as entering school in the fall. However, I continued to pray and trust in my God—the One who said "I am Alpha and Omega, the beginning and the end" (Rev. 21:6); the One who had parted the Red Sea and allowed His people to cross over to the other side on dry land; the God who promised, " 'And I will give thee the treasures of darkness, and hidden riches of secret places, that thou mayest know that I, the LORD, which call thee by thy name am the God of Israel' " (Isaiah 45:3).

In Habakkuk 2:3, the Lord told me that " 'the vision is yet for an appointed time, but at the end it shall speak, and not lie: though it tarry, wait for it; because it will surely come, it will not tarry.' " With all these promises, how could I worry?

The evangelistic meetings I was working with were coming to a close. A baptism was scheduled for the last Sabbath, and then the tent was to be taken down that same night. My last day on the job was to be August 22, and I began to wonder what I would do next. I had heard nothing more from Andrews. But for now I was busy completing Bible studies with prospective members and planning for the baptism.

The Friday before the baptism, I received a call from Andrews. It was the housing department. They told me that they had a three-bedroom apartment ready for me and that I could move in on August 23. A few days later, I received a letter of confirmation from the Genesis program welcoming me in. I praised God and rejoiced. He had everything planned, down to the very day. How could I ever have doubted?

chapter 23

Led Step by Step

My pastor, along with his family and some friends, volunteered to help us move from Connecticut to Andrews University. We arrived at 3:00 a.m. and quickly moved our meager belongings into the apartment before settling in for a little rest before dawn.

Later that same day, my friends left, and the children and I were alone. Thoughts of failure filled my mind, and I kept asking myself, "What am I doing here?" The reality of everything that had happened in my life over the past several years began to weigh heavily on my mind. Here we were in strange surroundings. And for the first time, the awesome thought of being solely responsible for my own welfare, as well as for my five children's, struck me like a bolt of lightning.

One thing I was certain of was that the Lord had promised to take care of us, and His promises are always sure. In fact, He sent many people to befriend us, and each day we were able to adjust a little more. There was ample time to get settled before my classes began and to help the children to get off to a good start in school. God made many provisions for us, and we could see His handiwork in our lives.

As the story about my experiences in Saudi Arabia and my testimony of the Lord's leading in my life became known, I could see that many were being encouraged by my experience.

I enrolled and began classes that same fall. The first quarter was very challenging. I had been out of the formal classroom for fifteen years, and I was very unsure of myself. I feared failure more than I feared anything else.

One night the Lord comforted me in a dream. I dreamed that I was outside of a building facing a very complicated stairway. As I looked at the stairway, I knew that I could not climb it; it was too difficult. All of a sudden I saw many students walking in with rulers, pencils, and books, and they started to climb the complicated stairway with no problems. I watched them in amazement, wondering how they could do it.

All of a sudden, I realized that I was not alone. There was a tall, stately figure by my side, who pointed another way for me. As he walked ahead of me, I followed. Every few steps, he would look back carefully, making sure I was keeping up with him. Everywhere he placed his hands, I placed mine; wherever he placed his feet, I placed my feet. Carefully and steadily we made it to the top.

It was with a sense of relief and accomplishment that I observed many young people receiving awards and, to my surprise, I was one of them. I later found myself in a beautiful home. The stately figure was still by my side. I became the owner of the building with the stairway. I looked out of the window and saw another person looking on with the same bewilderment that I had experienced when I first encountered the complicated stairway. I smiled and encouraged him, telling him that I was able to climb it and that I was sure that he could too.

I woke up from that dream with an assurance and a confidence that my degree had already been conferred on me; all I had to do was to persevere. I cried tears of joy as I realized that my God had deemed me an intelligent human being who had worth.

School continued to be a challenge, especially when coupled with my other responsibilities of being a single parent. But we were confident that God was leading us every step of the way. He provided for us and kept us faithful.

chapter 24

Created for Me

Day by day as I watched the children grow, I felt that they needed to have a loving father. My sons needed a good, strong, Christian, male parent to model before them how to be good, strong, Christian young men; and my girls needed the love that a Christian father could give. They had done nothing to deserve being fatherless.

Besides, I, too, longed for someone to love me and care for me and appreciate me for the woman that I was. I thought carefully about whether it would be best for a new husband and father to come into our home. It took all of two days for me to come to the conclusion that it would be a good thing for the children and me.

I started to pray about the matter earnestly every day. Then I began to pray every moment of the day. I joined a prayer group and asked the members to pray also. In my heart I believed that God had prepared me for a very special man. In my communion with God, I asked Him to create this man for me, because I knew that I was not completely healed from the effects of my experiences. I had suffered immensely and had some deep emotional scars. In spite of that, I felt that I had much to offer someone who truly loved the Lord.

I wanted a man who loved God more than he loved me and who had given his whole life to the work of the Lord. In my heart I was impressed that this person would have to be a minister for the Lord. I was convinced that what I was praying for was all a part of God's plan for my life, but I continued to dialogue with God about the matter. I wondered what people would think about a divorced woman with five children marrying a minister, and I questioned God about it. I wondered what kind of impact my past experience would have on his ministry, how it would affect his image. I talked to God constantly, expressing all my misgivings and my concerns. He comforted me by saying that I could ask anything in His name, according to His will, and He would give it to me. He led me to see that my marital breakup was as a result of a spiritual warfare, and He assured me that He would cover me and keep me from slander.

With this assurance, I started to ask God specifically to send me a minister. I felt the definite call to be a pastor's wife. I needed such a person whom I could speak to on a spiritual level; we could discuss beautiful spiritual themes together.

Fasting became a part of my prayer life. I continued fasting and praying for my husband. In faith I set the date for my wedding in June of 1993. It was now October, and I needed to meet my husband really soon in order to give us time to get to know each other before the wedding.

One morning as I was talking to the Lord, I reminded Him that there was not much time left before my June wedding and implored Him to do something really quickly. As I got up off my knees, I heard Him say to me, "You will meet him today."

I went through the day with a sense of expectation, but there was no knight in shining armor to meet me, and the day was drawing to a close uneventfully. However, I had one more function to attend—a rehearsal for a play I had volunteered to be a part of. I wondered about the man who would be the costar, so to speak. I had inquired about him and was told that he was a computer science major. Obviously, he was not the man for me. He was majoring in the wrong field. Nothing to look forward to, I thought.

Nonetheless, since this was my last opportunity that day to meet the man I would marry, I paid special attention to the way I looked before leaving my apartment. After all, who knew who would be at the rehearsal?

I made sure I was looking fine. My hair was together, face together, clothes together. Despite all my troubles, one of the things I never let slip was my appearance. I strongly believe that no matter what the test, as Christians, we should always do our best to be healthy and neat in our appearance.

When I arrived at the rehearsal, I started to go over my part. About half an hour later, the young man who had the part opposite mine walked in. We had never met. I eyed him as he walked down the aisle. He was a fine specimen! And very handsome too! And then it occurred to me, "He's a computer science major; what a shame!" Almost as quickly as that thought left my mind, another one entered. "Lord, do You think You could call him to the ministry before he graduates?"

The call to start rehearsing interrupted my thoughts. It was time to concentrate on my lines. The play was about Adam and Eve from the beginning of Creation down through the ages. I was Eve, and he was Adam. I watched as he was being created from the dust and recalled that my prayer to God was "Lord, create a man for me." I emerged from his side as his helpmeet. I felt a spiritual connection with my prayers as we went through the creation scenes. And, of course, the chemistry was right.

As we walked off the stage following the rehearsal, I sensed that he was quite impressed by my acting. He sought my advice on how best to do certain scenes. As we talked, I sensed that he was a very lovely person; but all I could think of was that he was a computer science major and hence not the one for me.

On our way toward the exit, we introduced ourselves somewhat belatedly. He asked me what my major was, and I told him social work. I asked him in return what his major was. The words came from his mouth as if in slow motion.

"Theology," he replied. The spiritual connection had come full circle and was now complete for me. What happened the next several moments remains a blur to me. My heart rang out praises to God, thanking Him for my husband.

At the time, Arthur did not know what God and I knew. God had told me in my morning devotion that I would meet my husband before the day ended. That is why the chemistry was so right. And that was the reason the strong spiritual connection was so tremendous when I saw my husband being created for me in the creation scene.

I floated to my apartment, walking on a cloud that night. My feet did not seem to touch the ground. I was beginning to feel like a complete woman again. And to be sure that I would be ready for my June wedding, I began reading everything I could find about Christian courtship. I wanted to know as much as I could about the roles and responsibilities of the husband and wife in a Christian home.

chapter 25

A June Bride

Most of the month of October was spent rehearsing for, focusing on, and producing the play. I said very little to Arthur, except in connection with the play.

On one occasion, I invited several of the members of the cast, including Arthur, to my home for dinner. My children fell in love with him. They interacted well together, without much effort, and he really seemed comfortable and at home with them.

The last performance of the play was tremendous. After the play, Arthur invited me to come to his apartment the next morning for breakfast. When I arrived, the table was exquisitely laid, and he served me a delicious breakfast—one that I will never forget.

Our friendship was established. We talked about the Lord much of the time; we were able to share spiritual thoughts at a level we both could benefit from. I asked him for his testimony about his decision to enter the ministry; I wanted to be sure he was truly called by the Lord. After hearing his story, I was assured.

Arthur called me every morning; we read Scripture and worshiped together over the telephone before we started our day. We complemented each other in every way; it was too good to be true!

Beyond the Veil of Darkness

As time went on, I began to get impatient with the Lord. Arthur had not proposed as yet. And then the Lord showed me that here was a man who truly loved God more than he loved me because he refused to make a decision about as sacred a sacrament as marriage without hearing from the Lord. And wasn't this what I had asked the Lord for? I praised Him for showing me my answer to prayer so clearly. I decided to wait patiently upon the Lord to confirm for Arthur what He had already confirmed for me. It was not as if a decision such as this could be taken lightly. Arthur had many things to consider—finances, the children (five of them to be exact), the fact that I had been married before, and a whole lot more.

A little more than three months after we met, Arthur proposed to me on January 22, 1993, but only after he had received confirmation after confirmation from the Lord. I later learned that he had agonized with the Lord over the decision and had received many definite answers in favor of our union. We were married on June 6, 1993.

Our marriage was made in heaven, as the saying goes; but it is more than a saying in our case. I continue to marvel at a God who is so interested in the affairs of men that He would pause to listen and answer the prayers of the least of His children. I have found that it is so important to have God choose your life's partner. I am a witness that God's way is always the best way. I've had it both ways, and His choice is better than mine, anytime. He will give you all and more than you ever ask for.

Arthur is a wonderful father to my children. They all call him Daddy. He is loving and patient and kind. He loves me dearly, and I love him dearly. I thank God for creating him just for me.

Epilogue

November 1997—Arthur and I have been married for four years, and it has been six years since my divorce from Mohamed. Arthur and I are both graduates of Andrews University, Arthur with a Master of Divinity and me with a Master of Social Work. God is great. Our children are in Christian schools; it's a struggle, but we believe in Christian education.

The children are now able to visit with Mohamed each summer. Or he may come here and visit with them at some holiday resort. The children are Christ's witnesses now to their father. Mohamed has a wife of five years and a daughter who is three years old. I give God thanks for my new life, for second chances, and for His forgiveness.

My brother Jeffery died April 26, 1997. He died in Christ, and now he awaits that great day of Christ's soon return.

To my dear children—I love you more than you will ever know, and I would give my life for you. I cannot wait for you to see Jesus and enjoy the heavenly sights that we have so long discussed. You will realize even more that your pain and suffering and all the sacrifices you made for Jesus were worth it, and you would not have had it any other way. Now that you are adults and young adults, find Jesus for yourself and keep

Him in your heart. You have nothing to fear except that you may forget the way that Christ has led you in the past.

To my brothers and my sisters (including the in-laws), thank you for your love and support and prayers. To my special sister-in-law, Merlene, I love you and thank you for being a pillar of strength for me.

To my brothers and sisters worldwide, my home church family in Gloucester, England, and Faith Church in Hartford, Connecticut, U.S. Thank you for your prayers and your lovingkindness to us.

To friends who cared enough to write to me and encourage me in Arabia, I will forever be indebted to you. Thank you.

To my darling mother, what a great lady you are—a true mother in Zion. I gained so much from your example. Thank you for all your prayers. And for believing!

To my husband, Arthur, thank you for your love and the appreciation you always give to me. It is so good to have someone by my side who loves the Lord as much as I do and is truly striving to see our family through to the kingdom. You are truly a priest in our home. I thank God for you each day.

Thank You, my God, for loving me so much and for Your patience toward me. Abide with me forever, for we have only just begun to walk together this strait and narrow road to Your kingdom. Keep me ever faithful, lest after sharing this beautiful testimony I become a castaway.... O Lord, have mercy on me.